# Books by K. C. Tessendorf

*Look Out! Here Comes the Stanley Steamer*
*Kill the Tsar!*
*Uncle Sam in Nicaragua*

*Uncle Sam in*

# NICARAGUA

# UNCLE SAM IN

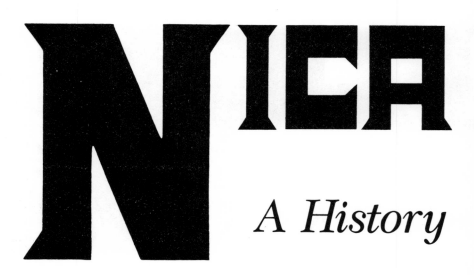

# NICA

## A History

ATHENEUM · 1 9

# RAGUA

*by K. C. Tessendorf*

8 7 · N E W   Y O R K

## PICTURE CREDITS

*Atheneum*
*Macmillan Publishing Company*
*866 Third Avenue, New York, NY 10022*
*Collier Macmillan Canada, Inc.*

*Composition by Haddon Craftsmen, Allentown, Pennsylvania*
*Printed and bound by Fairfield Graphics, Fairfield, Pennsylvania*
*Designed by Mary Ahern*
*First Edition*

*10  9  8  7  6  5  4  3  2  1*

---

*Library of Congress Cataloging-in-Publication Data*
*Tessendorf, K. C.*
*Uncle Sam in Nicaragua: A History*

*Bibliography: p. 131.*
*Includes index.*
*1. United States—Foreign relations—Nicaragua—Juvenile literature.*
*2. Nicaragua—Foreign relations—United States—Juvenile literature. I. Title.*
*E183.8.N5T47     1987     327.7307285     86-17340*
*ISBN 0-689-31286-5*

*TO*
*my scholarly predecessors*
*for developing a wealth of material*
*about U.S. and Nicaraguan activities*
*and personalities, and the national libraries*
*that have gathered and*
*preserved it.*

# Contents

# 1

# NICARAGUA

## *Getting to Know a U.S. "Tar-Baby"*

NICARAGUA, down in Central America; that country doesn't amount to much, does it? Oh, it's been in the headlines because some United States foreign policy experts claim that Nicaragua is full of communists who are trying to spread their influence all over the area and maybe the United States ought to be doing something about that. But isn't Nicaragua otherwise just a poor, dull, "banana republic" sort of place? Nothing much has ever happened there, has it?

Rich, Nicaragua has never been, or peaceful for long; but famous! You might be surprised. Over the years it has had more headline space in U.S. newspapers than any other Latin American country except Mexico and Cuba. Nicaragua is a crossroads kind of country, more so in the past than now, and it attracted at least passing attention from a lot of famous people:

Christopher Columbus discovered it; the conquistadores Cortés and de Soto wanted it; pirate Henry Morgan robbed it; Lord Nelson tried to take it for England; U.S.

presidents from James Monroe and John Quincy Adams right through to Ronald Reagan wondered and worried about Nicaragua. A herd of gold miners rushed through to California, and some stopped over to become fighting filibusters with adventurer William Walker, the free-lance American racist invader who briefly was president of Nicaragua. Financier Cornelius Vanderbilt chugged along Nicaraguan rivers and lakes and got richer. Two generations of future United States Marines generals received real combat training in its mountain jungles. Now and then such diverse personalities as writer Mark Twain and billionaire Howard Hughes stopped over.

Why did the United States have so much to do with Nicaragua? Geography was the reason. Nicaragua seemed to provide an easy crossing between the Atlantic and Pacific for Americans following their future to the west—or so it seemed for many years. U.S. relations with Nicaragua may be parodied as "The Wonderful Tar-Baby" story told by Uncle Remus. It was like this:

Brer Rabbit (Uncle Sam), he was hoppin' 'long, *lippity-clippity*, down *his* imperial road to where he thought he wanted to go, when there in his path, Brer Rabbit, he discovered a wonderful Tar-Baby (Nicaragua) sittin'. Brer Rabbit, he considered the Tar-Baby and how it might be put to profitable use. He asked questions but Tar-Baby ain't sayin' nuthin', Tar-Baby stay still. Meanwhile Brer Fox (the rest of the world), he lay low watching.

Brer Rabbit became vexed at the Tar-Baby's silence and inattention. "Sho'nuff, you're snotty, dat's w'at you is," says Brer Rabbit. "I'm gonna cure you, dat's w'at I'm gonna do." Brer Fox, he sorta chuckled in his stummick, he did, but Tar-Baby ain't sayin' nuthin'. "If you don't take off dat hat and tell me howdy," threatened Brer Rabbit, "I'm gonna bus' you wide open!" Tar-Baby stay still, Brer Fox lay low.

Brer Rabbit, he kept on askin', and the Tar-Baby, she kept on sayin' nuthin', till presently Brer Rabbit, he draw back with his fist and *smack!* hit Tar-Baby side of the face. His fist stuck to the tar; he couldn't pull it loose! "If you don't lemme loose, I'll knock you again!" says Brer Rabbit, and he soon did. Both hands were stuck now. "Turn me loose afor I kick the stuffin' outta you!" roared Brer Rabbit at the Tar-Baby, who said nuthin', did nuthin'. So Brer Rabbit, he then loss the use of his feet and could only butt with his head and so he got stuck all 'round. Then Brer Fox, he stepped out and invited Brer Rabbit to dinner, sayin' how he didn't see how Brer Rabbit could refuse!

Well, Uncle Sam, he was a big, tough rabbit. Nobody ate him up! With difficulty the United States pulled loose from the Nicaraguan tar-baby, leaving behind hide, blood, and treasure. It took about fifty years for the wounds to heal, to forget what a mess it was. Then in the mid-eighties, the U.S.A. began to think about whether or not to take another poke at the tar-baby, Nicaragua.

TO BEGIN, and to help understand the reason for U.S. interest, to see how it was and is, here is a crash course on Nicaragua's physical setting.

Nicaragua is the largest country in Central America, about the size of Iowa or a little smaller than New England, and it occupies a triangular wedge of tropic North America where the continent is slimming down. Nicaragua lies just 1,000 miles southwest of Miami. It can be reached in a jet plane in under two hours. The population is climbing toward three million, with 80 percent of its people concentrated in the western rim, about one-third of the land area. The eastern two-thirds is still wild and mostly uninhabited as it has always been, forgettable except for commercial timber, scattered mineral wealth, and as a base for guerrilla bands hiding out or preparing to take over the settled part of the country.

Drifting across Nicaragua from east to west, a balloon traveler would first see a swampy plain rising into three rugged east-west mountain ranges which to the west fuse into the continental divide, with six- to seven-thousand-foot peaks. On the west side lies an impressive geologic trench descending practically to sea level and containing at its south end the largest North American lake south of Chicago.

Lake Nicaragua, now close to and once part of the Pacific Ocean (it still contains large sharks that have adapted to fresh water), is one hundred miles long, forty-five miles wide, and features smoking volcanoes here and there on its shores and islands. Twenty miles to the north is the smaller but substantial Lake Managua. The three principal cities lie in the trench: Granada to the south, Managua between the lakes, and León to the north. A brief, narrow volcanic mountain chain rims the western edge of the country and shields it from the nearby Pacific Ocean. This ridge falls away on either end to low saddles, making easy land routes for lake-to-ocean commerce, with the lake and ocean only about a dozen miles apart.

Peering to the south, the airborne voyager sees the San Juan River, a navigable stream that drains the lakes at the southeast edge and flows east for about one hundred miles into the Caribbean. It was the possibility, never fulfilled, of an ocean-to-ocean commercial waterway from the Caribbean via the San Juan River to the lakes, with a short canal dug through to the Pacific, that, from earliest times, attracted the attention of powerful nations far away, especially the United States.

Man has probably lived beside the Nicaraguan lakes since his first arrival in the western hemisphere. Little is known of this until the rise, to the northward, of the energetic Aztec nation during the fourteenth century. At that time the lakeside dwellers were the northernmost members of the Chibcha tribe, based in present-day Colombia.

It was the Aztecs who first upset the political balance in Nicaragua. As they became powerful and thereby rich, they came to want emerald jewelry even more than plentiful gold ornamentation. But the emerald source was far away in the Chibcha heartland. So a mixed military and trade expedition came down to the lakes and easily subdued the local tribes. One of the tribes allied itself with the Aztecs and a permanent trading base was established. Chibcha emeralds trickled northward and the Aztecs responded with gold plate and ornaments.

This cooperative arrangement of trade, occupation, racial union, and cultural mixing seems to have lasted until just after the fateful voyages of Columbus. In 1502, Columbus briefly paused on the east coast of Nicaragua and was not impressed. He missed the San Juan River opening and the opportunity to sail up to the lakes. He passed south and found Costa Rica much more interesting.

Within a few years, though, the natives on the lakes noted an abrupt change in their foreign relations. Trade halted from the Aztec homeland, which was under attack by the Spaniard Hernando Cortés and his men searching for riches. Soon they were also isolated from the Chibcha, for Spain had occupied the isthmus of Panama. Of course the Spaniards learned of the lakeside enclave, and in 1522, under Gil Gonzalez de Avila, a typical Spanish raiding expedition came up from Panama. Soon a permanent settlement expedition arrived to complete the conquest and seek more gold. Christianization and a mixing with the surviving natives proceeded with success. Colonial Nicaragua became totally Roman Catholic and the people mostly a mixture of the two races.

The first Spanish explorations in the Americas were directed and ruled from Spain, but personal greed and jealousy of power were common among the adventurers. It was every man for his own empire. So, at the dawn of its colonial history, Nicaragua witnessed its first revolution.

The leader of the occupation in Nicaragua, Francisco Hernandez de Cordoba, was unwilling to send the lake-colony wealth back to Panama. He wanted it for himself. So Hernandez de Cordoba sent an envoy north to Cortes in Mexico to try and cut a better deal. But it didn't work out fast enough. One of his officers who did not agree with the double-cross was Hernando de Soto, the future discoverer and explorer of the Mississippi River. De Soto escaped from custody and, with others, slogged back to Panama. A Panamanian army arrived at the lakes ahead of troops from Cortes, who was then in Honduras, and the rebel Hernandez de Cordoba got his head chopped off.

The Spaniards did not find much more gold in the colony, and so they had to settle down and work for a living—that is, to compel others to work for them—raising cattle, growing crops of cacao, indigo, sugar. They founded the town of Granada beside the Nicarao Indian village and over centuries became a wealthy and conservative provincial aristocracy.

Galleons from Cadiz, Spain, sailed directly up the San Juan and across Lake Nicaragua to the docks and warehouses of Granada. Spain sent over an engineer, Gallisteo, to survey a canal cut through to the Pacific. But when the engineer determined that the lake level was a hundred feet higher than that of the ocean, the project was abandoned.

Though Granada was rich, it was not Spain's provincial capital. The governor had his seat in León, a city strategically placed near the principal Pacific port (most local travel was along the Pacific coast). Colonial administration was firmly controlled from the homeland and only *peninsulares,*

persons from Spain, were named to the overseas government. So León exuded an overseas, modestly cosmopolitan
(hence liberal) flavor, while Granada, saturated with creoles,
the local-born gentlefolk, had a conservative, inward-look-
ing atmosphere. This deep division of attitudes would, in the
future, spark many revolutions and battles and interfere
severely with the nation's destiny.

For the lake valley aristocrats, three hundred years
passed in pleasant money-getting monotony. This self-satis-
faction was interrupted occasionally by earthquakes shaking
and adjusting the geologically unsettled zone. A harsh quake
in 1663 drove up the bed of the San Juan River, making it
too shallow for the galleons. Now and again there were other
shocks to the local economy—terrible pirate raids.

The buccaneers attacked from both coasts. Sometimes
they were beaten off, but both Granada and León were
sacked and burned on occasion. The pirates were British,
French, Dutch—especially British. The young Henry Morgan was a successful raider upon Granada in his first foreign
foray as a buccaneer captain.

As a runaway Welsh teenager Morgan was kidnapped in
the British port of Bristol and sold into bondage on the
English Caribbean outpost island of Barbados. He did not
despair, and soon became adept at the loose and violent
ways of getting ahead. He escaped his master and joined a
British expedition against Spanish Santo Domingo, proving
his valor and leadership potential there and on the island of
Jamaica, where aptitude and opportunity made him into a
buccaneer captain before he turned thirty.

In 1664 Morgan joined other buccaneer captains in an
opportunistic raid on Central America. The pirate expedition cruised down the Mosquito Coast, wild jungle lowlands
along Central America's east side including Nicaragua, raiding and looting the Spanish trading posts. They found willing allies among the local Miskito Indians who hated the

Spaniards. The Miskitos told Morgan and company about Granada. Nicaragua's richest town then numbered 3,000 persons and supported seven churches.

Together the pirates and Indians rowed up the San Juan River and fell upon unsuspecting Granada by stealth and darkness. They penned up three hundred citizens in the cathedral and looted the warehouses, churches, and residences for a day and a half. The spoil was far more than the one hundred raiders could carry away. Having sunk all the local Spanish boats, the buccaneers and Indians boarded their own craft, leaving the hostages impoverished but alive. The savages had desired a slaughter, but Morgan intervened. The laden canoes barged down the San Juan to the sea, where the buccaneers transferred the loot to their own ships and returned to Jamaica in triumph.

In time Granada prospered anew. And after this promising beginning Morgan went on to spectacular plunders, favorable publicity, and eventual respectability. England's Charles II made him Sir Henry Morgan and appointed him to high government office in the newly British Jamaica. The gloriously expended pirate died in bed of tuberculosis and alcoholism at fifty-three. Morgan had been rewarded because successful buccaneers were, in the hands of overseas English leaders, valued tools for war and trade advantage. Whether their activities had secret approval or open official direction depended on Britain's status of war or peace with Spain.

After the English seized Jamaica, pirate intrusions were used to establish a British presence along the Mosquito Coast. (Already, in 1655, a Dutch pirate, Bleufeldt, had his base here on the coast at the site of the present port of Bluefields.) The British post was recovered by Spain and lost again. As the Spanish naval power weakened in the Caribbean, the English trading posts became permanent. The local Indians, the Miskito tribe, preferred English traders.

They paid better prices than the stingy Spanish trade monopoly allowed. Expanding their settlement slightly, the British laid out plantations worked by Jamaican slaves. Runaway blacks began an ethnic mix with the Moskitos, and "Mosquitia" was encouraged toward independence. Spanish Nicaragua, in the west over the mountains, did nothing effective about it.

In 1780, when England and Spain were again at war, an ill-conceived British expedition was sent out from Jamaica to capture the rest of Nicaragua. The Royal Navy man assigned to command transportation of the troops was a promising stripling named Horatio Nelson, then barely twenty years old. A small frigate was his first ship command. He was not consulted in the planning of the attack.

Everything went wrong. The expedition depended on help from the Indians, but they fled into the interior thinking the force wanted to transport them to Jamaican slavery. Finally Nelson succeeded in coaxing and bribing a minimum number out of the bush to aid them on the San Juan River approach. But it was near the end of the dry season and the river was extremely low. Their slow, slogging advance upstream halted before an earth and brush fort. The Spaniards had fortified the San Juan route.

The army commander cautiously wanted to settle down to siege tactics. Nelson, who later became England's most celebrated naval hero by defeating Napoleon's fleet, didn't think much of the breastwork and proposed immediate attack. Setting action to advice young Nelson began the assault by leaping, sword thrusting forward, from the boat's prow into the shallow water, where he sank to his ankles in mud. From this embarrassingly immobile position he writhed free, losing his shoes in the ooze. Barefoot, he led the attack, splashing and staggering forward to mount the crude battery in triumph. The fort had been abandoned by the sentries to these unexpected and crazy British. There were better forts upstream, and the Spaniards knew the tropical jungle was their strongest ally.

Already fever and dysentery were sapping the English strength and will. A sick Nelson was recalled to Jamaica and had to return to England for long recuperation. The doomed expedition was wiped out by fever and washed out by the onset of the rainy season. Of the two hundred navy men who sailed with Nelson, one hundred forty-five died of the dreaded yellow fever, which they called Yellow Jack.

Twenty-five years later, Admiral Lord Nelson gave his life in ending the emperor Napoleon's naval power at the sea fight called Trafalgar. The actions of Napoleon in Europe were the cause of Nicaragua's and many other more important Latin American Spanish colonies' move toward unexpected independence. If it weren't for Napoleon they might have remained Spanish colonial backwaters for yet another century.

In 1808 Napoleon invaded Spain and toppled its royal house, including the colonial administration. The Emperor's brother Joseph was set as a puppet on the throne. No Spaniard at home or abroad could stomach that. Then a British army landed in Spain and attempted to drive out the French and a modern constitutional monarchy was established.

Left to themselves while Spain was busy with the Napoleonic conquests, the colonies learned the basics of self-government and the military means to preserve it. Later when the restored legitimate Spanish monarch foolishly attempted to regain total control, the colonies successfully defied him and defeated the armies that he sent to America.

None of these stirring events happened in Nicaragua or nearby. It wasn't until the very end in 1821 that the colonial administration of the region, in Guatemala City, threw off the Spanish yoke in a peaceful transition. Immediately, however, an army marched down from the north, intent on rolling up the whole of Central America into the Mexican

Empire. But that would-be Central American Napoleon, Agustin de Iturbide, was overthrown in a revolution a year later.

The Mexican general who was in charge of occupation forces in Guatemala now had his opportunity. Vicente Filisola, an Italian soldier, probably could have become king or dictator of Central America. But General Filisola was a man both wise and prudent, more so than any other to appear on this scene in the next century plus. The general instead marched his army back to Mexico. The provinces of Guatemala, San Salvador, Honduras, Nicaragua, and Costa Rica were truly free nations in 1823. What did they make of this freedom?

# 2

## THE DOOMED
## CONFEDERATION
### *National and Diplomatic Futility*

LATIN AMERICA, emerging from colonial status to independence from 1808 through 1823, was inspired by democratic idealism and chose the United States as its role model. Certainly the new republics looked for support and early recognition of their nation status by their big-brother republic to the north. They did not get it. The go-slow mood of the United States was tied to self-interest. The recent War of 1812 had been a near disaster and the postwar attitude was that of caution regarding any entanglement with a large European nation. Also, there was opportunity for U.S. territorial expansion, and that came first.

The new republics were viewed coolly. To revolt was one thing, but to remain free was another. What if the United States embraced a new nation and then Spain took it back? Very sticky—especially since the U.S. was then engaged in delicate, slow-moving negotiations with Spain to obtain Florida. The U.S. played it safe and waited until the final expulsion of Spanish forces had occurred around 1821.

No one in official Washington in that year worried about

our foreign relations with Central America. It was a blank spot on the map until it thrust itself into the State Department's consciousness in 1822 when a delegation from a could-be nation called El Salvador turned up in the capital. They were desperate men. Rather than become a part of Mexico they offered their country to the USA:

> *And You, heroic people of the north of America! You who see in every man a brother, and in every American a being worthy of your assistance, do not reject our vows: admit us to your bosom: extend your protection to a people till now oppressed, who wish to be free; and shelter them from new attacks of tyranny.*

But Secretary of State John Quincy Adams would have none of this flattery and appeal. The well-traveled son of a president, himself a president-to-be, shrewdly held a low estimate of the prospects for democracy and peace within the new republics. "Arbitrary power, military and ecclesiastical, was stamped upon their habits and upon all their institutions," Adams wrote. "Civil dissension was infused into all their seminal principles." With polite blandness he shunted aside the Salvadorans.

The year 1825 would be the final one of James Monroe's presidency. He was the last and least charismatic of the Virginia line of founding presidents. By the middle of his second term, it was apparent that Monroe had not scored a great triumph as a statesman. It would be personally gratifying if he could finish with a bit of a flourish.

Monroe's inspiration began in an Englishman's brain. George Canning, the British prime minister, was thinking about Latin American trade and how Britain would profit now that the Spanish monopoly was ended. Yet the French and Spanish were reported to be considering a joint effort at reconquest of the area. Perhaps they could be warned off, and it would be useful if the United States joined in the English declaration of purpose.

The proposal reached President Monroe in the August of 1823. Quickly and cautiously he queried ex-presidents Jefferson and Madison: *The British want us to join them in declaring that the new republics be upheld, and that no new European political penetration of Latin America be allowed. What do you think?* The elder statesmen agreed it was an inspiration profitable to American interests and would also strengthen Anglo-American relations in this "era of good feeling" at home and abroad. So Monroe would likely have gone along with Britain, except for the inspiration of his Secretary of State.

The feisty John Quincy Adams declared that there was now an opportunity for America to distinguish itself before the world and not just follow "as a cock-boat in the wake of the British man-of-war." He convinced the president, who, in his last major address, told Europe that the United States would view as "dangerous to our peace and safety" any new interference by the Old World in the affairs of this entire hemisphere. In return Monroe pledged that the U.S. would not interfere in Old World politics or fight in its wars.

So the United States went it alone. Canning was furious at being upstaged by the upstart new nation. Britain and the others scorned the declaration, saying they would continue to do as they pleased in the New World. But what England wanted was the trade advantage offered by this flock of new independent nations. So it came to be that it was the British fleet that was the real guarantor against recolonization by France and Spain.

James Monroe thus left office with his desired popular triumph. The United States was not militarily able to enforce its new principle, but had a peeved silent partner in Great Britain. The Monroe Doctrine had been enunciated and was there as a tool for bold future presidents of a stronger America to shape and use as befitted their situation.

In 1824 Secretary Adams read in a newspaper some detail about the Central American Confederation, a union of Guatemala, El Salvador, Honduras, Nicaragua, and Costa Rica that came about following the withdrawal of Mexico from their lands. The secretary of state remembered that the president of the confederation, Manuel Arce, was one of the Salvadorans who had met with him a year past. Adams believed it was worth looking into. There was some American trade with that region, and if a preferential trade treaty were negotiated it should increase. He recalled that the British were well installed along the Mosquito Coast. It would be prudent to keep an eye on them.

Adams picked as trade representative to the confederation a North Carolinian, Thomas Mann, a plain-spoken type who asked, in effect: *Fine; what is it, where is it, and how do I get there?* At the State Department they pointed out the vicinity of Guatemala City on their world globe. But they didn't know anything about the country or how to get there. The new diplomat was referred to the U.S. Navy. Quite a while later he boarded a navy vessel at Norfolk, Virginia, and then died of a stroke before it sailed. Another Carolinian, William Miller, an ex-governor, was recruited. He reached Key West, Florida, with the navy, where he contracted yellow fever and died. Meanwhile an envoy from the confederation had arrived and was seeking a syndicate to complete a commercial waterway across Nicaragua.

In April of 1826, John Williams, a rugged army veteran from Tennessee, set out for Central America, taking along a clerk. Pausing at Havana, Cuba, they heard lurid tales of the terrible trail from the sea over the tropic mountains to Guatemala City—of the horrid climate, insects, fevers, jaguars and pumas, mountain chasms, and gangs of bandits—a fearful gauntlet. The clerk quit, but Williams persevered and arrived unscathed in the capital in late May.

What had happened to the host nation in the two years that the United States had been attempting to place its man on the scene?

The Confederación Centroamericana was doomed— though it would stagger on for years—by the unrelenting hostility of its Conservative and Liberal factions. The democratic process is fiction if one party will not abide being governed by its opponent, or if the party in power uses its position to deprive, exile, or imprison the opposition.

If the Conservatives had had their way, there would never have been a confederation. They favored an exclusive union of the aristocracy with the church in a monarchy modeled on the Spanish Middle Ages. But the Liberals— lawyers, merchants, teachers, the middle class—had surprised and outmaneuvered them and were now in control of the confederation. The Conservatives were, however, gaining influence by luring the Liberal president into their camp.

The newly arrived American diplomat saw a government shaken by increasing disturbances. The spirit of the times was: Do it our way or get your lumps from us! A revolution was coming on, and sensing this, the pragmatic U.S. envoy worked doggedly to push the trade treaty through the distracted Congress before the government exploded. He succeeded in obtaining a trade treaty in which each nation reduced its tariffs by one half to the other. Williams posted the document to the Department of State and enclosed a plea for a navy ship to take him home. Three months of Central American politics were too much for him.

As the disgusted Williams prudently slipped down to exit via the lakes and the San Juan River, the Liberal-turned-Conservative President Arce imprisoned the Liberal state governor of Guatemala, a conservative stronghold, and immediately another prominent Liberal politician was murdered in the countryside, torn apart by a crazed mob before the altar in a church he had fled to. Then the Liberal-dominated state of El Salvador rose in revolt, leading to a war that seesawed for several years.

What about Nicaragua? It was worse there! That state had hardly participated in Confederation politics because the Conservatives and Liberals at home were so antagonistic and evenly balanced that they kept this unhappy land in nearly perpetual warfare between 1823 and 1835. Twice troops from the Confederation entered Nicaragua to pacify the country, but as soon as an emergency elsewhere (and there were plenty) drew them away, the ingrained conflicts flared again.

It took a natural disaster to temporarily slow the pace of Nicaraguan warfare. In 1835 the volcano Cosiguina, one of the hot spots in the seaside rim of the lake trench, blew its top. The resulting cloud obscured the sun and rained down sandy powder that reeked of sulphur. This condition worsened over three days. Then, in the words of an observer:

> *A loud detonation, followed by heavy shocks of earthquake, rain of sand, and total darkness, rendered the terror of the people complete. Flocks of birds fell dead to the ground and wild animals sought refuge in buildings. The frightened inhabitants ran to their yards, or hurried to the churches to implore divine mercy. . . . The parish priests in several towns, during the prevailing darkness, preached from their pulpits that this shaking of the earth was a manifestation of God's wrath for the crimes of the Liberals. . . . Forty-three hours passed before the earth became quiet, when a strong wind cleared the atmosphere, enabling the people to ascertain the damage.*

The years 1835 and 1836 were calm, vaguely progressive years in quake-shocked Nicaragua. But in 1837 the political kinds of eruptions began again, leaving their debris of human suffering and economic ruin. Conditions had returned to normal.

In groping toward some understanding of Nicaragua's compulsion toward civil anarchy, it is helpful to comprehend two "ismos" prevalent in Latin American social relations:

*Personalismo:* Emphasis on the pride and dignity of the individual. Personal relations with others are delicately set and maintained. They are of far more interest and importance than attention or allegiance to a national society. Personal feelings and local contacts shape political attitudes and activities.

*Machismo:* Cultivation of a male's feelings of supremacy, with emphasis on displays of self-confidence and success in sexuality and random social encounters with other males. There is an inability to accept a public defeat, however slight.

Linked with these attitudes or poses is the preference for a family connection in every social or economic activity.

The only operating national organization in Nicaragua was the very conservative Roman Catholic church, the bond between the wealthy and the poor. In every town and village the church's servant, the priest, was regarded by the peasants as the authority or man of wisdom. The local paternalism was well meant on behalf of the rural individual, but in these conditions, national pride in the modern sense was nonexistent in about 90 percent of the population.

In the United States Henry Clay had become secretary of state. He sought to place another American diplomat in this theater of chaos called Central America. The man he chose turned out to be an artful dodger. William Rochester was in Mexico City when appointed in the spring of 1827, but quailed at the prospect of entering the strife-torn next-door country. Instead, he made tracks in the opposite direction. In June he was in New Orleans, supposedly arranging southern passage, but in July he was back at home in upstate New York. He kept Washington regularly informed of his plans to proceed, and needs for money, but Rochester did not sail on a navy ship until a year after his appointment.

The USS *Falmouth* made a leisurely circuit of the Caribbean before placing the envoy ashore, briefly, in Central America. The devious diplomat quickly ingested all the local gossip about the dangerous and anarchic conditions inland. Quickly reembarking, he wrote a long report about it as he returned to the United States. Acting on this intelligence, Secretary Clay severed U.S. diplomatic ties with Central America, and none the wiser, wrote Rochester a letter of commendation.

There now arose, in the civil war of the confederation, Francisco Morazan, a Honduran general who won a series of battles on behalf of the Liberals and, in 1830, pierced the Conservative heartland and captured Guatemala City. The conservative way of life took a beating under liberal victors.

The new regime struck hardest at the alliance of church and state. The Roman Catholic church was severed from the government. Its assets were taken over, its seminaries and monasteries closed. The haughty church hierarchy was rounded up, trekked across the wild mountains to the Caribbean, and jammed aboard a ship for a one-way passage to Spanish Cuba. The hardships of the journey caused several deaths.

In 1831, as the seething Conservatives were absorbing their hard knocks and plotting a new overturn, the United States decided to send a representative to the Morazan government. William Jeffers was quite willing to proceed. But a political enemy revealed him as a bail-jumper from a felony charge some years past. By order of President Andrew Jackson he was arrested as he was awaiting his ship at Pensacola, Florida.

The following year, Kentuckian William Shannon, the innocent of these annals, set out for Central America, taking along his wife, son, and a teenaged niece. They very much enjoyed their navy voyage into ignorance and peril. Shannon's last letter is filled with the sort of dutiful praise for crew and food that satisfied cruise passengers write. But within a few days of landing he and the niece fell suddenly and fatally ill of fever and were buried in an unmarked jungle grave, and the distraught survivors took refuge with the British consul back at the port.

In 1833, the tireless Department of State, "the position of Chargé now being vacant," picked on a former congressman. New Yorker Charles DeWitt, a prickly and morose individual, was no optimist. When he learned what had happened to the Shannons he became laggard about departure and tried to avoid Central America as long as possible. He told the State Department that he planned to sail around Cape Horn to Santiago, Chile, then work his way north along the Pacific coast. They pointed out he would be twice as far from his destination in Santiago as he was in New York! So, bitterly protesting, DeWitt traveled the standard route, survived the terrible trip to the capital, and settled in for a five-year stay, the last three years of which were involuntary.

DeWitt was not a stellar envoy or reporter for the United States. He seems not to have stirred from Guatemala City, except by necessity at the very end. He did not follow the Liberal government when it fell back to El Salvador. His occasional reports to Washington are boring and basically meaningless. "Tranquility" was a term he often used. He guessed that the British were behaving benignly. But by staying so long at Guatemala City (he had received permission to leave but was too timid to proceed), he gained firsthand knowledge of the Carrera phenomenon or terror.

The Conservatives planned to return to power via an Indian uprising. The hinterland of Guatemala was thickly populated with Indians who were fervid Catholics. An anti-Liberal–antiforeigner campaign was started successfully among them. It became unwise for officials or strangers to venture far outside the capital. Guerrilla warfare began, and General Morazan was unable to crush it.

A startling Indian leader emerged. He was illiterate Rafael Carrera, then twenty-one, whose last occupation was that of swineherd. But among the guerrillas he displayed a terrible charisma, and his Conservative advisers watched out for him. As his fame expanded among the Indians he became known as "Rafael the Avenging Angel." It was reported that at a large meeting in a church where Carrera was present, a letter fluttered down from the rafters. It was read out to be a political endorsement of the leader from the Virgin Mary!

Again a natural disaster had a political repercussion. A plague of cholera swept the land in 1837. The Morazan government made a genuine effort to provide aid, sending medical teams into the countryside. The team members washed their surgical instruments in the streams. Word spread that these strangers were thereby poisoning the Indian population. Bands of Indians seized several doctors and forced them to drink all liquids in their possession. Since this included laudanum (opium-alcohol solution) they invariably died, thus confirming ignorant suspicion. The Conservatives picked up the tune, noting that Morazan had encouraged European settlement (in the empty eastern jungles), and the propagandists claimed that a plan was afoot to kill off the Indians and replace them with gringos, (white) foreigners.

On a frenzied tide of antiforeign hysteria Carrera's ill-disciplined forces invaded Guatemala City. An outraged Liberal observer reported:

> *It is fearful to recall the continued assaults on the houses into which through doors and windows the roving soldiery fired their arms killing and wounding the unresisting occupants without regard to age or sex. . . . All this time the Conservatives enjoyed immunity beneath the shadow of the monster. He received the homage of the noblesse . . . and in the great cathedral he was impiously proclaimed as an angel sent of God!*

The youthful Carrera is recalled as attired in "coarse frieze trousers, a fine coat with gold embroidery, and a woman's hat with a green veil."

Though envoy DeWitt had declared in an old-fashioned flourish: "If I must perish, let me perish in the house of the North American Legation beneath the flag of the United States," he spent the worst of this period hidden in a closet in the house of "two respectable widows living nearby." Fortunately, Carrera's political overseers influenced him to leave town, and the horde retired to the Indian heartland with all the spoil that they could carry.

DeWitt, now in a hurry to get out of the country, was stunned by the coincidental arrival of a command from another world—Washington, D.C.: *Our trade treaty is expiring. Don't return without a renewal!* He tried his best. He journeyed in peril to El Salvador and induced one house of the congress to extend the treaty, but before the other did so a political upheaval scattered the assembly. His only hope now was President Morazan's signature, but the general was having trouble with Carrera and was beyond reach of the despairing negotiator.

In March 1839, DeWitt appeared in Washington. Secretary of State Forsyth asked for the treaty. It was, said DeWitt in guilty evasion, in his trunk at Gadsby's hotel. Forsyth chatted on: Now that the treaty was ratified it had been decided to close the legation at Guatemala City and he, Charles DeWitt, must shortly return there to do it.

It was too much! He would be considered a failure for returning without the treaty; and then to face the long, dangerous road back into chaos. . . . They just didn't understand. The poor soul took his own life.

Back in Central America, Carrera gathered his Indian army and moved out from guerrilla tactics to field confrontation with the Liberal army, which he pushed back. Nicaragua then declared its withdrawal from the fiction of the Confederación Centroamericana and other member states followed. Fifteen years of chaos and civil strife—143 recorded battles—were closed out. President General Morazan fled to South America. Attempting a comeback several years later, he died facing a firing squad in Costa Rica.

Guatemala soon stabilized under Carrera, who cruelly and efficiently matured into a terrible caudillo (Latin American despot) and ruled harshly until his death nearly thirty years later. Nicaragua tottered along, contentious and strife-torn as ever. It had set itself up as a modern republic with a shiny new constitution, elected government and all. But former habits were difficult to break. Latin American historian Dana Munro aptly describes the debilitation of democracy:

> *The elections soon became a farce because of the ignorance and indifference of the great mass of the people. The history of the Central Americans had never taught them respect for the will of the majority, and there was consequently little inclination from the first to accept an unsatisfactory verdict at the polls in good faith. The authorities*

*gradually learned to bring pressure to bear upon the voters in the interests of the party in power, and as time went on assumed a more and more complete control of the balloting, until candidates opposed by the government ceased to have any chance of success.*

*At the same time the members of the opposition party were restrained or expelled from the country, to prevent their intriguing or revolting against the government. Within a few years authority established and upheld by force was the only authority which was recognized or respected, and there was no means of changing the officials in power . . . except revolution. Civil war had thus become an indispensable part of the political system.*

In Nicaragua the next decade saw multiple internal Conservative-Liberal overturns and external wars with El Salvador and Honduras. The resident English diplomat, Frederick Chatfield, badgered the financially ruined nation to pay back its share to the British bankers who had foolishly lent money to the defunct Confederation. And Great Britain rudely asserted its claims to the east coast of Nicaragua and insulted the powerless new nation by kidnapping the would-be governor of the disputed area.

The United States knew or cared very little about all this. Two more envoys appraised the area, at great personal risk, in 1839 and in 1841. They reported no twitch of life in the confederation. Then the U.S. abandoned diplomatic contact with the area for six years. If another misfire appointee be counted—the burned-out editor who took the job on his deathbed in the belief that the tropical climate would mend his health—well then, there had been ten American diplomats . . . and now there were none. It had all been a glaring example of diplomatic futility.

But this cautious attitude in overseas policy ceased in the 1840s. America was on a winning roll of territorial expansion: Texas, Oregon, and then, as war spoil, from Mexico, the New Southwest, and California, all acquired in three years! The proudest buzz words of that decade became "Manifest Destiny!" America was God-chosen to overspread the continent, and beyond, because its was the fittest race.

President Polk, in 1848, fresh from beating up Mexico, grandly expanded the Monroe Doctrine by warning that if a third power threatened a nation of the western hemisphere, the U.S. might be compelled to occupy that country for its own good.

Also, in 1848, gold in quantity was discovered in California, setting off a major get-rich-quick migration. It took several months to cross the USA in a wagon. It was much quicker, and in some sections more comfortable, to travel by ship to Panama, or closer still to cross Nicaragua, and sail again to the Golden Gate. It looked like there was a lot of money to be made in Nicaragua. Moneyed and political interests focused on the area and on Great Britain, now jealously considered a potent rival there. During the next decade Nicaragua would be hard put to maintain its shaky independence.

# 3

## NICARAGUA SMOTHERED!

### *Financiers, Filibusters, Gunboat Diplomacy*

THE GREAT territorial outreach of the United States was watched with jealousy and disapproval by Great Britain. The English were not at this time themselves interested in colonizing the Americas, but they were very sensitive to trade advantage and did not want to be pushed around in the New World by the Americans. The British government, led by Lord Palmerston, fussed over which country over-confident "Brother Jonathan" (the USA) might gobble up next. When the quickest sea-land route to the California goldfields was scouted as by way of Nicaragua, the British schemed to slow the United States by paramilitary blockage of the route.

England was well set up in eastern Central America through its puppet kingdom, Mosquitia, and its true colony of British Honduras (now Belize) below Mexico's Yucatán peninsula. Mosquitia spread rather haphazardly through the jungled Caribbean lowlands of Honduras and Nicaragua. Its frontiers were vague: wherever British fancy placed them. Mosquitia was an Amerindian-black tribal monarchy. Its compliant line of kings sat at British selection, each of whom was crowned in comic-opera coronation ceremonies in Belize city. The present king, Robert Charles Frederick, lolled in rustic and boozy luxury in the capital village of Bluefields on the central east Nicaraguan coast.

The dreary little shack town of San Juan del Norte at the mouth of the San Juan River lay about one hundred miles below Bluefields. Suddenly it was strategically important as the port of entry for the crossing of Nicaragua. Cleverly England prodded Mosquitia to stretch itself southward to include the river port. British gunboats, on Mosquitia's behalf, expelled the Nicaraguan officials in 1848. But after the warships sailed away, Nicaraguan troops stubbornly reoccupied the town. Then three hundred British marines landed, routed the small Nicaraguan force, and in the track of the British pirate Henry Morgan boldly moved up the San Juan into Lake Nicaragua. As Granada, hometown of the aristocrats, was sure to be occupied next, helpless Nicaragua hastened to agree that Greytown (San Juan del Norte) belonged to King Frederick's Mosquitia. Britain had a fist over one end of the soon-to-be-popular Gold Rush shortcut.

For many years Britain had been well served by its peppery envoy in Central America, Frederick Chatfield. The aging bachelor was short, rotund, very imperial in manner. Chatfield's obsession was Britain's diplomatic position in Central America, which he passionately believed was of supreme importance to England's foreign policy. Chatfield had lined up firm allies in Guatemala and Costa Rica. But Honduras and Nicaragua, imposed on by Mosquitia, and El Salvador, which worked to the opposite of whatever its enemy Guatemala was doing, were anti-British.

In 1849 the rigid envoy of England was matched by an eager and effective envoy from the United States, Ephraim George Squier, a very bright archeologist, young man of the world, and true believer in America's manifest destiny. Left to themselves, these two self-important zealots might have embroiled their nations in hotheaded war.

Squier's instructions from the Taylor administration included negotiation of a canal and passenger-transit treaty with Nicaragua. The flashy steamboat tycoon and Wall Street financier Cornelius Vanderbilt desired this concession. And "Commodore" Vanderbilt was respected as a man who got what he wanted. Nicaragua, buffeted by Britain, wanted a protector and clutched at the United States. So Squier easily obtained an exclusive treaty, which wrapped up the passage across Nicaragua for the USA. But it also involved America as Nicaragua's guardian, far exceeding Squier's instructions.

Chatfield sizzled and reacted sharply to this move to Americanize his turf. He pushed Costa Rica to dispute its northern border with Nicaragua, to claim the south bank of the San Juan River and the south shore of Lake Nicaragua. Next Chatfield considered how a British plug might be stuck into the western exit-entry. Chatfield supposed that the canal-passenger route might follow the lake trench to its northern ocean edge on the Gulf of Fonseca, international waters bordered by Honduras and El Salvador as well as Nicaragua.

A Honduran island in the gulf, Tigre, could support an English naval base commanding the Pacific entry to the waterway. Honduras owed British bankers sizable debts. On his own Chatfield offered to have his government assume their payment in exchange for obtaining Isla de Tigre. The aggressive diplomat wished to jam up the U.S. canal transit at both ends, and maybe in the middle, too.

But U.S. envoy Squier was also on the scene, negotiating an eighteen-month American lease of Tigre Island. Squier, handsome and suave, was by far the more popular diplomat. Also, a British gunboat had just trashed the Honduran east coast port of Trujillo during a Mosquitia-type dispute. So, assuredly, in October 1849, Squier got his lease. As soon as Chatfield knew this was so, he contacted the nearest vessel of the English Pacific fleet to approach Tigre Island. The day after the official announcement in favor of the United States, the British Navy and Mr. Chatfield ceremoniously occupied the disputed island.

Now it was Squier's turn to be outraged, and for the cause of peace it was a good thing that he did not have a U.S. warship at hand to commandeer. But while Squier sputtered at the arrogant power play of his rival, the British admiral commanding in the Pacific cautiously overruled his subordinate and to Chatfield's discomfiture the English forces were soon withdrawn from Tigre—which Squier promptly "occupied" by seeing to it that the Stars and Stripes were lifted above it.

What did all of this tit-for-tat barbed diplomacy amount to when the word trickled back to Washington and London? Was either nation willing to fight for its Central American position?

Of course, there was much chauvinistic outrage in the press on both sides of the Atlantic. But the governments damped the explosiveness by quietly disavowing the actions of their own envoys. Chatfield and Squier had both magnified their positions and exceeded their instructions. To Great Britain, the Central American lands were a third-rate diplomatic theater. But Lord Palmerston knew that the Americans were more anxious. They wanted the Nicaraguan transit as well as the Panamanian. He saw here an opportunity and sent to Washington one of his slickest diplomats. Henry Lytton Bulwer was to negotiate a safety valve over all Central American disputes and in doing so mildly put one over on the canal-crazed Americans.

The subtle Mr. Bulwer was fortunate in encountering an American negotiator who was not a rabid, manifest-destiny expansionist. President Taylor's secretary of state, John

M. Clayton, was of a restrained attitude toward territorial aspirations. As a senator he had even voted against the United States' annexation of Texas. To the English envoy's questions about U.S. intent to take over Central America, and particularly Nicaragua, Clayton answered firmly in the negative.

Then Bulwer soothingly intimated that neither did England want to colonize further in that area. Yes, and Great Britain understood the American desire for a Nicaraguan canal transit route to its new western states. Such a project could be a great commercial boon and therefore should benefit all nations, or at least England equally with the United States.

Each diplomat retained an ace to play in the game:

Mr. Vanderbilt was eager to install his canal. But though he was the second-richest man in America he would still have to borrow a great deal to fund his transisthmus ditch. Both Bulwer and Clayton realized that only the wealth of Britain could help.

Clayton's card was a dangerous one, and probably a bluff. He reminded the Briton how angry citizens and politicians were about British highhandedness in and around Nicaragua. Then he displayed Squier's treaty with all its exclusive, protective provisions. How would Mr. Bulwer like to see it pushed through the Senate? He would not.

So the text of the Clayton-Bulwer Treaty of 1850 was composed. It guaranteed Anglo-American cooperation and oversight of any transisthmian canal. There would be no fortification or colonization in the future by either Great Britain or the United States.

In recommending the treaty, Secretary Clayton believed that British encroachment in Central America would cease and (ignoring Nicaragua) there would not be any more trouble about transportation right-of-way there. Though the partnership didn't fit a manifest destiny type of Monroe

Doctrine, all would be well as the British cleared out of the area.

The ratifying U.S. Senate surely believed that Britain had agreed to pull out of Central America. But England afterward held firm to an interpretation (the Bulwer treaty wording was slippery) that it was committed only on future moves. Past territorial acquisitions remained in place (and Greytown was Mosquitian!). Clayton absorbed much punishment on this point of unexpected British advantage. The other setback came when Mr. Vanderbilt went over to England to finance the Nicaraguan Canal. The London bankers wouldn't budge—Clayton-Bulwer or not.

So Great Britain scored in restraining runaway American expansion impulses, at least the official ones, and gave up little since it had no grand Central American schemes anyhow. It was a valuable and trusted contract, though, to hold to in the disturbed period immediately ahead in Nicaragua. It defused the possibility of mistaken war between the Atlantic powers, which over this area would have been truly silly and dreadful.

As dispenser of canal concessions, Nicaragua had been a generous host. The crinkly, white parchment documents emblazoned with pretty red, blue, or gold medallion seals had been repeatedly issued to American and European syndicates.

Engineers, some legitimate professionals and others frauds, occasionally surveyed the route and came up with vastly differing estimates as to technique and cost. In any of the schemes the amount of investment capital demanded was very great by nineteenth-century standards. It was impractical to round up that much money, and foolish to dump it into the unstable political mess of Nicaragua. That was why none of the several franchise holders ever collided in Nicaragua, waving their duplicate canal contracts.

Cornelius Vanderbilt was no dreamer, nor had he

been born yesterday. As his origins had been dirt poor and his formal education scanty, so had his business success been astounding. His father, a struggling farmer on Staten Island, New York, had begun a part-time small ferry service to Manhattan. Young "Corneel" took it over, improved and expanded the service, and vastly extended the ferry business. He thrived so in this hardheaded and hardhearted enterprise that he achieved the nickname of "Commodore" after coming into control of most of the water traffic roundabout New York. The ferry profits were managed with spectacular success in the stock market as Vanderbilt emerged as an authentic native tycoon and financier of that era.

He was in energetic middle age at the time of his Nicaraguan venture. Persons meeting or observing the Commodore remembered him well. He was tall, handsome, loud and profane, proud of being lowbrow, brash but shrewd, a ruthless charmer, flashy. In self-confidence he knew no superior.

Vanderbilt accepted the British turndown of his canal-financing proposal with aplomb and pushed forward his passenger transit plans for Nicaragua. He may have expected the English rejection. Commodore Vanderbilt's interest in Nicaragua was in carrying gold miners to and from California and thereby getting richer himself.

Operating a passenger line from New York via Nicaragua to San Francisco called for planning ahead and resources behind. Otherwise it might go as the earlier "Gordon's California Association" charter trip did—very slowly and painfully.

In the dawn of gold-rush hysteria in February 1849, promoter George Gordon chartered a sailing ship *Mary,* advertised the journey via Nicaragua at two hundred sixty dollars a head, and secured a shipload of gold seekers. At Greytown, the expedition produced from the ship's hold the parts for its own river steamer. A good move, but it took a long time to put it together and get it in operating shape. Eventually they chugged up the San Juan for a while but found they could not get past its rapids. There was a delay of three weeks in getting around them on foot and then arranging native boat transfer to the western side of Lake Nicaragua. There was further delay before the miners rode on muleback over the ridge to the Pacific Ocean.

No scheduled ship awaited them and they lingered a long time in Nicaragua before desperately crowding aboard the first ship to finally put into port there, the slow and decrepit *Mary Ann,* which couldn't cope and went to shore along the deserts of Baja California. The travelers nearly starved before the chance arrival of another ship. It was a full eight months before these exhausted travelers limped in through the Golden Gate.

Cornelius Vanderbilt did it a lot better. He would operate frequent connecting ship services on both oceans. He went ahead himself and prepared the way. Aboard his large new steamship *Prometheus,* the Commodore sailed down to Nicaragua in June 1851. He was on his way to Granada to expand his canal concession into a transportation monopoly called the Accessory Transit Company.

But his engineers intervened with a problem. They, like Gordon, could not get their river steamer, the *Director,* past the San Juan rapids. According to his biographer, the challenged and enraged Vanderbilt reacted in fine style:

> *"Hell's delight," he howled, "I never see sech a passel of lazy, wuthless suckers. It's costin' me five thousand dollars a day to sit 'round here and smack the skeeters off. Now, I'll tell ye somethin', the lot of ye. Thar ain't goin' to be more foolin'. We're goin' up that San Jew-on to the Lake, if I have to tow the* Director *myself."*

*The engineers protested volubly. They didn't
mind the fallen trees and the sand bars and the
inhospitable alligators; but it simply wasn't possible
to pass the worst rapids. Of course, if the
Commodore wished it, they could dig canals—*

*"Canals, my eye," roared Corneel. "I'm through
with canals. This is goin' to be a steamboat line. Fust
ye steam up, and then ye steam down. That's all thar
is to it. Git aboard, and I'll show ye how."*

*He embarked a crew of thirty men on the*
Director, *borrowed plenty of stout cable from the*
Prometheus, *and steamed into the San Juan, fuming
and cussing. The men who accompanied him spoke
of their experience afterward with awe.*

It was a harrowing trip. With the Commodore navigat-
ing, the crew, at his order, tied down the safety valve and
at maximum pressure repeatedly "jumped" the river rocks,
the wooden-hulled vessel groaning and tearing alarmingly.
Sometimes they would have to get out the cable, loop it
around a sturdy tree on the bank upstream, and with a steam
winch wind in the cable, thereby drawing the vessel against
extreme river currents. They made it through to the lake,
as Corneel never doubted. And so having proved his point
at great threat to life and ship, Vanderbilt directed it not be
done again. He had his steamers arrive at either side of the
worst rapids, which were then navigated by passengers and
freight in safe shallow-draft barges.

Cornelius Vanderbilt proceeded upon his mission to
Granada and it was a triumph.

Vanderbilt paid Nicaragua ten thousand dollars a year
for exclusive use of the ocean-to-ocean transit. He was supposed to share a small portion of his profits with that nation,

too. But the books were kept far away in New York and the accounts scrambled so that they never showed a company profit, though it was boasted elsewhere that a profit of a million a year was not unusual.

Though he was gruffly cordial to the officials at Granada, he regarded the lot, based on their evident lack of national progress, as leaders of an inferior race. This would be the characteristic view of many American businessmen, diplomats, and soldiers in Nicaragua over the next century and more. The land and the natives were there to be used, and to the extent that this usage helped them, well, fine!

Before he left Nicaragua in November, the Commodore had personally set up the operations of the Accessory Transit Company. It was Vanderbilt all the way—his steamers sailed from New York to Greytown, on the San Juan River and Lake Nicaragua. He chose Virgen Bay on the west bank of the lake as his land terminus and directed that a company installation be built there. Over the shortest route, twelve miles, a true road was constructed across the rim of the mountains and down to the Pacific, where he laid out his own port at San Juan del Sur. Eventually the road was hard-surfaced and comfortable coaches moved the passengers across. Vanderbilt steamers completed the link to California.

Just as the energetic financier and developer was departing Greytown to New York aboard *Prometheus*, a nasty international incident occurred. The Mosquitia proprietors at Greytown collected a port usage tax. All ships paid except those of the Vanderbilt Line, whose captains persistently denied the authority of Mosquitia.

Aware that the owner of the shipping line was aboard, the officials decided to press the issue. Vanderbilt vowed that he would not pay unless forced to. The customs man returned with several police. The Commodore ordered them off his ship, blustered that there were desert islands along the route where they could be marooned if they lingered. Shoved off the ship by impatient passengers and crew, the police complained to the British consul, probably by prearrangement.

The English warship *Express* was in port and was ordered to detain the *Prometheus,* already on its way out. There was no response to the warship's command signal to halt. *BOOM!* A solid ball passed over the bow of the *Prometheus* and another crossed the stern low enough for passengers lounging there to be fanned by the breeze of its passage. The *Express* signaled that the next shot would be shrapnel into the center of the steamer. The *Prometheus* turned back and a livid Commodore Vanderbilt paid. He had been forced.

The American government handled this hot potato by protesting vigorously to London, at the same time sending a warship to Greytown to inform the British consul that he was in violation of the Clayton-Bulwer Treaty. The U.S. did not contest the port tax. The British government disavowed the actions of its servants and the issue faded.

Commodore Vanderbilt took his revenge by causing his own company town to be built across the river, thereby ending the opportunity of Greytown merchants to profit from his Accessory Transit Company. Matters simmered into 1854 when Greytown officials began boldly molesting Vanderbilt personnel and destroying company buildings. In relief, the U.S. warship *Cyane* arrived and left behind a guard at the company town. The atmosphere was ugly and soon inflamed by another incident.

A Vanderbilt steamer coming down the river collided with a native-operated boat. The resulting dispute became superheated and ended with the American captain, Smith, shooting and killing the native. U.S. Ambassador Borland, as hotheaded and chauvinistic as the captain, witnessed the episode and justified the action. When Greytown police attempted to arrest Captain Smith, the "diplomat" Borland pointed a rifle at them saying he meant business. They withdrew.

The ambassador foolishly went ashore that evening to visit the American commercial representative. A menacing mob tried to "arrest" the belligerent envoy. He was struck in the head by a chunk of broken bottle. During the night his escape to the ship was managed and so in high dudgeon he reported his version of the incidents to Washington.

This time, when the American sloop of war *Cyane* returned to Greytown, a classic action of "gunboat diplomacy" was played out. Commander Hollins sent ashore a demand for twenty-four thousand dollars' "damages" and waited—but not very long. There being no reply he messaged that he was authorized to destroy Greytown and offered shelter of the *Cyane* to anyone desiring refuge. A few came aboard while everyone else fled, most into the surrounding jungle.

There was a minor British warship in port to which the English ran. The *Bermuda* messaged that it regretted very much that it was too small to fight the *Cyane*. After expiration of the deadline, the *Cyane* bombarded empty Greytown to pieces and sent U.S. Marines ashore to torch the shreds.

Great Britain was at this time tied down in its Crimean War. Also, its expanding textile industry relied vitally on cotton from the American South. Possibly consideration of these factors entered into the planning of the *Cyane*'s action. To the English protest the State Department smoothly replied that they regretted Commander Hollins had exceeded his instructions. But had he? Not likely! Those who crossed Commodore Vanderbilt did not get away with it for long.

Greytown, weedlike, quickly sprang up in shacks again. The British positioned a good-sized gunboat there, and torpid peace resumed along the Mosquito Coast.

The occasional clashes at Greytown were minor skits compared with the main show over the mountains in the main area of Nicaragua where the populace continued to erupt as often as their volcanos. The Conservatives had managed to stay in power a few years, then reneged on a promised shift of power. Thereupon the Liberals revolted. The self-destructive contest seesawed between the rival citadels of Conservative Granada and Liberal León. Vanderbilt's transit route lay to one side and the passage of *los Yanquis* was generally not affected.

Some of Vanderbilt's travelers fitted well the description "adventurer." They had abandoned normal pursuits in a dash and grab for California's gold. Most of them failed to get rich; and some of these did not want to go home again. They had not extinguished their wanderlust or their hope for romantic, enriching adventure. The Nicaraguans began attracting these to their ragtag armies.

At Vanderbilt's Pacific port of San Juan del Sur open recruiting flourished. Restless Americans could enlist in either the Conservative or Liberal armies. Hard cash being scarce, the lure was usually in sharing the spoils of war following victory, perhaps a country hacienda. Meanwhile, there was raw glory to be had, and booze and senoritas. Scores of Americans and Europeans signed up and got their gritty adventure, sometimes shooting at one another and dying for it. These foreign soldiers of fortune were called filibusters in those days.

The Nicaraguan leaders were impressed with their performance. Frequently the filibuster supplied personal weapons far superior to average Central American arms. Many were Mexican War veterans who brought good ideas of form and strategy into combat. And especially there was the adventurer's innate self-confidence. He trusted that he was better than a dozen of the "degraded" natives and attempted to prove it by being steadfast in battle.

In 1855 a fatal suggestion came to Francisco Castellon, leader of the Liberal insurgents. Why not hire an army of filibusters wholesale? They'd really sock it to Granada, then! Byron Cole, a visiting Californian, was the evil genius promoting this scheme. The present Liberal government of neighboring Honduras had granted his syndicate a valuable mining concession. Cole believed that this obliging government, and his commercial advantage, would collapse if the Liberal revolt in Nicaragua failed. Also, he reasoned, if Castellon won he would remember and reward Cole for his potent advice.

Castellon thought it was a splendid idea. And Cole said he knew the man who could do it. He was William Walker, a "grey-eyed man of destiny," who would organize such an army in California, bring it into Nicaragua and lead it to victory. So it was that this scourge upon the land came not by invasion but by Nicaraguan invitation.

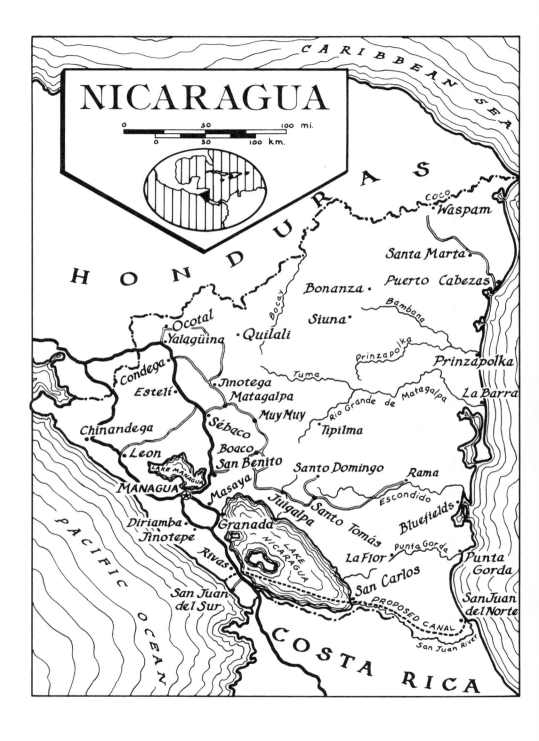

# NICARAGUA

0    50    100 mi.
0    50    100 km.

CARIBBEAN SEA

HONDURAS

COCO
Waspam

Santa Marta

Bonanza    Puerto Cabezas

Ocotal    Siuna    Bambana
Yalagüina    Quilali

Bocay

Prinzapolka    Prinzapolka

Condega    Tuma    La Barra
Estelí    Jinotega
Matagalpa    Rio Grande de Matagalpa

Chinandega    MuyMuy
Sébaco    Tipilma
Boaco
Leon    San Benito    Santo Domingo    Rama
Lake Managua    Escondido
MANAGUA    Masaya    Bluefields

Diriamba    Juigalpa    Santo Tomás    Punta Gorda
Jinotepe    Granada    La Flor    Punta
Rivas    LAKE NICARAGUA    San Carlos    Gorda

PACIFIC OCEAN    San Juan    SanJuan
del Sur    PROPOSED CANAL    del Norte
San Juan River

COSTA    RICA

*John Quincy Adams, as
Secretary of State, turned
down the offer to annex
part of Central America
to the United States*

*Americans, lured to California by the discovery of gold there, found
the trip across Nicaragua the quickest route to the West Coast. Here
some travelers stop for breakfast on the shores of Lake Nicaragua.*

*Commodore Vanderbilt. Cornelius Vanderbilt was in energetic middle age at the time of his Nicaraguan venture.*

*William Walker, Nicaragua's Yanqui misfortune—"The Gray-Eyed Man of Destiny."*

*Philander C. Knox, U.S. Secretary of State with the corporate outlook. He was founder of Dollar Diplomacy and destabilizer of President Zelaya.*

*Jose Santos Zelaya ruled Nicaragua absolutely for sixteen years.*

SEÑOR DON ADOLFO DIAZ,
President of the Republic of Nicaragua.

*Adolfo Diaz: The mining clerk who bankrolled the anti-Zelaya revolution with $600,000!*

*Major Smedley D. Butler. This shrewd, plain-spoken Marine's Marine saved the anti-Zelaya revolution and established the American presence in Nicaragua.*

# 4

## THE BOGUS MAN
## OF DESTINY

### *With William Walker*
### *in Nicaragua*

WILLIAM WALKER, Nicaragua's future unfortunate
"grey-eyed man of destiny," was born in 1824, the eldest of
four, into a pious upper middle class family in Nashville,
Tennessee. The small, thin, freckle-faced lad's manners
were correct from the first. "He was very intelligent and as
refined in his feelings as a girl," approvingly recalled a
neighbor. "I used often to go to see his mother and always
found him entertaining her in some way." Mrs. Walker was
a semi-invalid whom William waited on devotedly.

Young Walker earned good grades at school, scrupled to
always say and do the right things by adult standards. He did
not join in with other boys in fooling around and mildly
reproved companions who did. He was on the whole un-
naturally serious. Walker was not a sissy, but he was a grind
who graduated from the University of Tennessee at age
fourteen.

His parents intended him for religion, but William instead chose medicine and obtained his degree from the University of Pennsylvania. He traveled to Europe to continue his medical studies. But there the young man decided that a career of doctoring was not his preference after all. He lingered abroad another eighteen months, traveling, observing, trying to figure out his future. Walker remained a socially withdrawn moralist. He disapproved of big-city European life-styles and frivolity. It was a lonely time, but he may have been so self-centered as not to have minded that.

Returning to Nashville in 1845, he turned to law and mastered a degree. He chose lively New Orleans to begin lawyering. Though he excelled in book learning, he was not social enough to prosper in the legal profession. People respected William Walker (no one called him Bill), noting intelligence, courage, resolution. But the man was no mixer, rarely even chatted, and few could recall having seen him smile.

Walker soon sidestepped from law into journalism (editing, not reporting) and felt comfortable at this distance from his readers. His printed views were fairly liberal for the South, not notably pro-slavery.

At twenty-four William Walker fell in love, a novel opening of his persona not to be repeated. The woman was Ellen Galt Martin, vivacious, beautiful, and a deaf mute. The five-foot-four-inch, 120-pound editor applied himself with his usual success to mastering sign language and pleaded his love convincingly. The enthralled couple set their wedding date. But in 1849 Ellen, only 23, died as a cholera epidemic raced through New Orleans.

He submerged his grief beneath his former gravity of face and manner, but his personality altered as he groped for a way to compensate for the shock to his soul. This was the time in national affairs when everything focused on golden California. And William Walker was lured with the rest.

Walker did not scratch in the Sierras for gold nuggets. He became one of the merchant-professionals in San Francisco who received gold secondhand from the miners, resuming a mixed career of newspaper editing and lawyering. As a publicist he was a good deal more contentious than in the past and embroiled himself in civic disputes. He survived a duel or two. He evolved into something of a leader on the far-out fringe of U.S. imperialism. And he became a doer, not just a talker.

The Pacific beaches marked the physical end to American continental expansion. But the habit and the desire of Americans for new lands to occupy remained at full tide. To the north, vigorous Canada backed by Great Britain offered no takeover possibility. But to the south—ah, that was different! It seemed there were at least a dozen warm, fertile lands down there with untapped mineral wealth. And their native populations did not amount to much; the weak governments could be easily managed or eliminated. To imperialistic dreamers growing stale beside the Golden Gate, it seemed like a vacuum that must be filled by superior outsiders like themselves.

At this time a province of northern Mexico, Sonora, seen through a haze of distance, seemed alluring. There were rich silver mines in Sonora and probably much other undiscovered treasure. But the central government at distant Mexico City was too weak to militarily cope with the savage Apache Indian attacks on settlers and miners that had isolated the province. General Santa Anna wanted this silver safeguarded and devised a plan of European (*no* Americans allowed) settlement that would also present a buffer against *Yanqui* encroachment from the north. This scheme degenerated into two invading filibuster expeditions recruited from displaced French adventurers in California. Both were absolute disasters from which neither of the leaders returned alive.

It was into this cactus-studded and guerrilla-infested desert trap that William Walker, having organized a colonization syndicate with the money of gullible Californians, now inserted himself with a ragtag group of luckless followers.

Somehow the years of self-contemplation gave Walker the assurance that he was destined to take over, rule, and improve, with white men's genes and skilled oversight, some mongrel nation to the south. Manifest Destiny often prompted manifest delusion. The audacity of this individual without political experience or backing deciding to be a man of destiny is a remarkable phenomenon.

A Guatemalan general, Zavala, told of Walker's moral habits in Nicaragua, shrewdly observed: "If [Walker] doesn't drink, smoke, or have any devotion to Bacchus or Venus, it is clear that the only thing he desires is the sensuality of power." Walker had found his compensation.

A description of Walker, made during a preliminary undercover visit to Guaymas, the port of Sonora, has been preserved:

> *His appearance was anything else than [that of] a military chieftain. Below the medium height, and very slim, I should hardly imagine him to weigh over a hundred pounds. His hair light and towy, while his almost white eyebrows and lashes concealed a seemingly pupilless, grey, cold eye, and his face was a mass of yellow freckles, the whole expression very heavy. His dress was scarcely less remarkable than his person. His head was surmounted by a huge white fur hat, whose long knap waved with the breeze, which, together with a very ill-made, short-waisted blue coat, with gilt buttons, and a pair of grey, strapless pantaloons, made up the ensemble of as unprepossessing-looking*

*a person as one would meet in a day's walk. . . .*
*Indeed half the dread which the Mexicans had of*
*filibusters vanished when they saw this their Grand*
*Sachem—such an insignificant looking specimen.*

*But anyone who estimated Mr. Walker by his*
*personal appearance made a great mistake.*
*Extremely taciturn, he would sit for an hour in*
*company without opening his lips; but once*
*interested he arrested your attention with the first*
*word he uttered, and as he proceeded, you felt*
*convinced that he was no ordinary person.*

It must have been a personal magnetism coupled with the
absolute confidence with which he outlined his views and
plans that attracted and held tough, failed adventurers and
rough down-and-outers. Here was their second or third
chance, probably their last, to ride along to glory and power.
How fortunate they felt to meet and be enlisted in the cause
of this man of destiny!

Walker had trouble getting his Sonora filibustering expedition out of California. U.S. officials were on to him and
realized his plans were in violation of neutrality laws. In
October 1853 he managed to get away, though with only
forty-five recruits, most of them the scum of the San Francisco waterfront. Walker realized that he could not achieve
Sonoran conquest with this inadequate force; somewhere he
must await reinforcement. So he invaded Baja California,
captured its undefended capital of La Paz, and imprisoned
the governor. Then the ambitious filibuster proclaimed the
region's independence and made himself president—he
planned to rule two Mexican states instead of one. The locals
didn't understand what was going on, but that did not matter because Walker departed as suddenly as he had appeared. The marauders sailed northward and moved into

the port of Ensenada in the upper section of Lower California. There they waited for more men and supplies.

Word of William Walker's "conquest" in Baja California attracted two hundred thirty avid filibusters, who arrived well stocked with anticipation but with little food. The troops began foraging at the scattered desert ranches, driving off cattle. Rural robbery provoked the victims to arm themselves and go after the thieves. Harassed by the ranchers and on tight rations, the fainthearted abandoned destiny for an eighty-mile hike back to the States. Meanwhile Mexicans conspired and stole Walker's ship.

In a desperate maneuver, the flailing filibuster marched his shrinking "army" across the peninsula toward Sonora. Cattle were driven along for food and his men raided for supplies wherever any existed, against outraged inhabitants who fought back with guerrilla-type attacks. The exhausted American band managed to get across the broad Colorado River and finally and briefly into the desert waste of that part of Sonora. But their remaining cattle drowned. Even as Walker grandly proclaimed Sonora his "independent republic," the expeditionary force collapsed from physical distress and began an unmilitary retreat toward the U.S. border at Tijuana.

As thirty-four ragged, bootless survivors trudged toward the boundary, a line of horsemen from the Mexican guerrilla force that had harassed them for weeks sneeringly blocked their passage. Walker, never lacking grit, rallied his hard core into a desperate, staggering, screaming charge. Startled, the Mexican cordon divided before them and the filibusters tottered on into U.S. custody. When Walker surrendered, he signed himself in as "President of the Republic of Sonora." It was May 8, 1854, William's thirtieth birthday.

Why didn't this fiasco eliminate permanently the pretensions of William Walker? His disgrace was real, but a lot of Californians wanted to believe otherwise. Some acclaimed him a hero; the jury favored him with acquittal of charges of interference with the sovereign right of Mexico.

Then Walker received the Nicaraguan invitation arranged by Byron Cole, his business associate, and outfitted himself to sail to Central America. But once again he had to sneak out of California with only a small group of recruits. Although after his acquittal the U.S. marshals ignored the filibuster's activities, Walker was in trouble because he came up short of funds to pay for his supplies. Creditors sought to hold Walker's vessel as security. The latter fixed his famed eyes upon the sheriff's deputy guarding the ship and cajoled and bribed him. So he and the sparse force he later praised as "the fifty-eight immortals" escaped aboard the slow, old *Vesta,* which took fully six weeks to reach the port of El Realejo in the Liberal-held part of Nicaragua. The grateful Americans filed off on June 16, 1855, and the allies looked each other over.

As the Nicaraguans had expected, these bearded *Yanqui* soldiers looked and acted bigger than life size. They were tall, extremely self-confident fellows, clad in red or blue flannel shirts, coarse miner's trousers, and boots. Their broad black felt hats were tipped at a jaunty angle. The arms they carried were super too—modern, efficient rifles, revolvers, bowie knives. Sworn in as Nicaraguans, they were named the American phalanx and Walker was appointed a colonel in the Liberal army.

The Americans looked contemptuously on the tattered specimens of the Nicaraguan Liberal army. The puny, barefoot, brown soldiers carried ancient, worn-out muskets. Many were ignorant, dispirited draftees. The only thing uniform about them was their small stature and general look of malnutrition. But their leader, General Jose Muñoz, was stuffed importantly into a gold-braided red-and-blue uniform and was so fat he looked like a multicolored balloon. Walker and Muñoz were not going to get on well.

Muñoz was intent on attacking the Conservative army and eventually capturing Granada. From command jealousy he planned to scatter the Americans among units of his own army. Walker insisted on his separate command of the filibusters and told the Liberal brass that he had his own war plans. He must at once occupy the passenger transit line to ensure a steady flow of recruits and supplies.

Applying his charismatic powers, Walker pushed his plan to attack and occupy Rivas, a provincial center near the western end of Vanderbilt's route. Finally General Muñoz consented, perhaps treacherously. He agreed to send along a Liberal unit of one hundred ten troops to aid in the attack.

The *Vesta* ferried the force southward and landed them at night in swampy jungle for a two-day muddy hike and climb over the ridge toward inland Rivas. A Conservative army of five hundred men was expecting them. Walker's plan was simple: Charge into town and penetrate to and hold the central plaza. The fifty-eight "immortals," rallying one another with confident cheers, rushed into the enemy stronghold. As the filibusters charged, their Liberal allies scattered, running in the opposite direction. This placed the immortals in a terrible fix at the short end of an eight-to-one manpower ratio.

Battle momentum carried Walker and the fifty-eight up a house-lined street, but stalled short of the plaza. The filibusters sheltered in several homes from which they cracked out a killing defense, being by far the superior sharpshooters. Walker's casualties were fifteen and included two of his top associates. Then the enemy thought to set fire to the grass roofs. Driven out by flames, the Americans had to leave behind five wounded as with wild yells and a grand show of revolver shooting they dashed out of the town with only one further casualty. Though they had killed many of the Rivas defenders, their first effort was a defeat.

The discomfited American phalanx limped back to the

Liberal heartland, where they were further dismayed to learn that their wounded comrades in Rivas had been bound to a pile of wood and burned alive. Walker sent to President Castellon an accusation of Muñoz's treachery and bluffed that he would return to the States unless the general was punished. Castellon did not chastise Muñoz, but he was forced to allow Walker a free hand in determining strategy.

With a personally recruited native force of one hundred twenty that he hoped would be steadfast, Walker and his veterans sailed down to San Juan del Sur, Vanderbilt's Pacific port, and marched over the twelve-mile road to base themselves, with the complicity of two of Vanderbilt's associates, in the company installation at Virgen Bay on Lake Nicaragua. Immediately they were attacked by the vengeful Rivas army commanded by General Santos Guardiola, "the butcher of Honduras," who never took prisoners. Remembering the Rivas atrocity and with the lake at their backs, Americans and Nicaraguans both fought superbly and routed the attackers, who left sixty dead and numerous wounded while Walker's force was nearly untouched. At his order the surgeons cared for the enemy wounded, a practice Walker would always follow, though his native allies thought him crazy not to allow them to bayonet or shoot them in vengeful sport.

This victory established credence in the filibusters' power in Nicaragua. By October Walker's force, with new arrivals from America as well as more native recruiting, had increased to around two hundred fifty men. Now their grey-eyed leader put into motion his slickest operation. A thick guard was placed around Virgen Bay to immobilize spies. On the evening of October 12 Walker commandeered a Vanderbilt steamer and with a load of troops sailed forty miles up the lake and stealthily approached Granada. The filibuster raiders, just one hundred ten men, landed before dawn at the edge of the sleeping city and captured the

Conservatives' capital with ease and only slight bloodshed. Walker conquered with a few, where entire Liberal armies had failed for years. Huge headlines in the States!

Though the Conservatives' families were now Walker's hostages in Granada, General Ponciano Corral, the boss Conservative in the field, refused the conqueror's offer of negotiation. Then an unauthorized raid by Walker recruits occurred when they fired on a fort from a transit steamer. The nervous fort gunners then fired on another steamer, killing civilian travelers. Walker took a severe view of the incident. In reprisal he publicly executed the highest Conservative official he had captured, Mateo Mayorga, a cabinet minister. General Corral got the message that the tough filibuster would do the same to others in Granada until there was peace, and soon came in and agreed to a treaty. The bloodstained revolutionary merry-go-round halted briefly as the riders changed places. In the new government sat an elderly figurehead president, Patricio Rivas, with General Corral as minister of war. But General William Walker was the army commander-in-chief and thereby the strong man of the lot.

The treaty and new government were just two weeks old when Walker received proof that Minister of War Corral was only going through the motions. Letters Corral had written to other Central American leaders, imploring them to intervene and overturn the filibusters, were intercepted. At a cabinet meeting Walker fixed his coldest stare upon the traitor and laid out the evidence. Paling, the general accepted the accusation, and was court-martialed by the filibusters. He was shot in the main plaza of Granada on November 8.

Since the former Liberal President Castellon had died in a cholera epidemic during the war, and shifty General Muñoz had been killed in a battle, William Walker was alone at the top after only five months in the nation of Nicaragua.

Early success led into headstrong overconfidence and care-lessness. From this time just about everything he did was wrongheaded. Generally, it was the filibuster's ignorance and mishandling of foreign relations that united his enemies and aided them in ousting him from this tormented land within eighteen months.

By the time Walker ruled at Granada, the realization that he represented and promoted an alien race, that he was grafting an ethnic cancer upon their Hispanic heritage, was clear to other Central American chieftains. Walker would eliminate Conservatives and Liberals alike by overwhelming the traditional leaders with an imported master race. They knew they must collaborate to stop him.

Had William Walker been a clever "man of destiny" as well as a visionary one, he would have dispatched envoys to sooth their fears, to "stroke" them with promises or bribes. Better still, he would have utilized their chronic feuds and hatreds by arranging individual alliances and aiding in crushing their enemies with filibuster armies. He didn't have the foreign military muscle yet, but its filibusters were clamoring for passage to Nicaragua. Talking, stalling for just a few months, would have made the difference.

Instead Walker publicized his racist vision of a slavocracy in Nicaragua, then Central America, even Mexico (he'd rule Sonora yet!) and Spanish Cuba. When in 1856 Walker elevated himself by a fixed election to become President Walker, he changed national law to allow slavery. To the liberal world at large this was degenerative outrage and consolidated international opposition.

Walker offered white soldier-settlers two hundred fifty fertile acres apiece. Black slaves would be imported to work the white estates. He believed that blacks were more efficient workers than browns. It was not the filibuster's plan to rejuvenate the land and then offer it (like Texas) for U.S.

annexation. Walker sensed that the slave South was at its limit and would decline under the populous industrial North. Walker's mania was to found instead a new land for slavery.

This preachment of ethnic imperialism found plenty of believers, especially in the South. All over the United States this grandest filibuster was hot newspaper copy, the media champ of 1856. He came on strong as the grey-eyed knight of manifest destiny, as a popular prophet cursed or exalted but constantly in the public consciousness.

So in this crucial year of 1856, while President Walker faced a gathering of enemies on the perimeter of Nicaragua, a host of potential recruits yearned to come to him. The filibuster's worst blunder was to infuriate the man who could help or hinder him the most in transporting friends to his side.

Commodore Vanderbilt's New York–Nicaragua–California line prospered. Later, when Vanderbilt closed the Nicaraguan transit, the Commodore was so feared that steamship competitors paid him up to $56,000 a month to stay out of the California passenger business!

In 1854 Vanderbilt sold control of his California line to business associates Charles Morgan and Cornelius Garrison. But he retained a big block of stock and trusted they would be good stewards while he took a long vacation. He ordered construction of his grandest steam yacht, the *North Star,* and with his large family cruised over to summer in European seas and show off the accumulated wealth of American free enterprise. While the yachtsman frolicked, Morgan and Garrison maneuvered in the stock market to plunder the absent tycoon.

When the Commodore returned he was mightily upset and dictated to his secretary (who combed out the cuss words) this memorable declaration of corporate war:

*Gentlemen:*

*You have undertaken to cheat me. I will not sue you because the law takes too long. I will ruin you.*

*Sincerely yours,*
*Cornelius Van Derbilt*

It took the Commodore over a year to accomplish the strategy he chose, the quiet accumulation of voting stock in the company. In the meantime William Walker got sucked into the enemy camp.

Walker's credibility after winning the battle at Virgen Bay yielded him the friendship of Charles McDonald, the Transit Company's manager. So Walker did not have to steal the company steamer he used to capture Granada. Behind McDonald stood Morgan and Garrison, who foresaw that if Walker's white paradise was imposed upon Nicaragua it would be good for their business. Many more Americans would come to Nicaragua in addition to those passing through. At a critical time in the filibuster's campaign the Accessory Transit Company advanced him twenty thousand dollars. Walker was hooked.

When Vanderbilt regained company control in January of 1856, he was friendly for the same business reasons. He agreed to carry Walker recruits to Nicaragua for just twenty dollars a head. But Morgan and Garrison, now shoved outside, went to Walker and collected for their past favors. At their direction, using as cause the nonpayment of profits to Nicaragua, in February 1856 President Walker put Vanderbilt out of business inside Nicaragua and took over company steamers and installations. A new company of Morgan and Garrison's monopolized the transit right. They agreed to concentrate on ferrying to Nicaragua, gratis, the expanding numbers of recruits hankering for filibuster spoils and glory and otherwise supply William Walker's needs.

Vanderbilt's immediate reaction was to shut down his Atlantic and Pacific steamers. This isolated Walker for about six weeks until Morgan and Garrison got their own ocean vessels going. The Commodore's wrath was aroused: "Him and me are enemies. If it takes my last dollar, I'm agoin' to ruin that cheap tin-sojer in Nicaraguey, and git my own. You watch me!" The vengeful financier became the banker and armament supplier to all Central Americans willing to fight William Walker.

The harassed filibuster didn't need this type of vindictive attention. All through 1856 his position worsened. The grey-eyed man of destiny's only brilliant tactical stroke had been the surprise attack on Granada. Elsewhere he fumbled against his multiple military foes. Walker's simplistic idea of lancing into a town center sometimes caused encirclement and required a desperate charge to get out again.

Another Walker trait was absurd destruction. Instead of braving bullet-sprayed streets, he would order his troops to batter through successive inside house walls, burning the ruined dwellings behind them as they wrecked their way forward. Physical exhaustion overtook the Americans before they could reach the central plaza in this bludgeoning manner. The calculated destruction further lowered their reputation in the nation.

The northern Central American and Nicaraguan allies were based at León, while Costa Rica pressed from the south. Despite terrible plagues that killed thousands more than did filibuster bullets, and their intense internal bickering, the north-south offensive slowly pushed Walker back toward his Transit lifeline. Finally forced to abandon Granada, Walker ordered it destroyed and left a formidable rearguard force to do it. The residents were herded into the cathedral while for seventeen days drunken (from household stocks) filibusters attempted to carry out the order. Granada was solidly constructed of stone, so they did not entirely succeed before Walker returned on a steamer and rescued his exhausted vandals from the "smoky bedlam" of Nicaragua's proudest city.

Walker's sole hope was concentrated upon the swelling arrivals of starry-eyed recruits. He needed the lot of them in the struggle to stay even against losses to disease:

> *During . . . six weeks . . . about thirty of our company died, mostly of chills and fever, and at the end of three months, nearly all of our company had died. . . . The food was fresh beef and coffee; we had no salt or bread; I could eat but little of it and would go hungry till I could stand it no longer. . . . The men soon weakened by their fare and sickness and seemed discouraged at the prospects before them.*

An agent of the Commodore, Sylvanus Spencer, in early 1857 put the plug into the Nicaraguan Transit, thereby beginning the end of foreign involvement. Supported by Vanderbilt money and weaponry, Spencer organized and paid for a small Costa Rican army, which the former Transit engineer led to a surprise conquest of Walker forts on the San Juan River. Aboard captured steamers, he raided up and down the river and lake and held on. Morgan's and Garrison's ocean services shriveled; they were ruined. Vanderbilt was so pleased that he gave Spencer fifty thousand dollars (valued at a quarter million today).

Walker, isolated from reinforcement, soon holed up in Rivas, the mountain town where his military adventure had begun. In May 1857, near the second anniversary of the departure from California of the fifty-eight immortals, an arranged surrender put out his torch of white destiny. Walker and his staff departed under U.S. Navy escort; his troops were paroled into Costa Rica, disarmed, and shipped back to the States. One estimate places the sometime total of Walker's filibusters at about five thousand, with a casualty rate of about 50 percent.

As after the Sonoran fiasco, the gray-eyed visionary had been hailed in the States as a hero. It was widely expected that he would now soon reenter that nation of which he was, in name, "President." Walker tried twice and was foiled by the elements, and then once by the U.S. Navy, which intercepted his landing at Greytown. The American government had hesitated, delayed, done nothing effective about the Walker phenomenon—until it was obvious that he was a loser.

The filibuster's popularity faded amid the failures. In a last effort to return to his "constituency," with a force of one hundred he attempted to get at Nicaragua via Honduras but stalled there. A British naval vessel "rescued" him, but when Walker insisted that he was not an American citizen, rather the wrongfully deposed president of Nicaragua, the British turned him over to Honduran control. The local commander sent a messenger to the capital to ask what to do with the prisoner. The president of Honduras was General Santos Guardiola, "the butcher of Honduras" and Walker's late, unforgiving adversary.

On September 11, 1860, William Walker, then thirty-six, stoically looked into the musket muzzles of a squad of the ragged, barefoot brown soldiers he had come to Central America to displace. Their volley killed the bogus man of destiny, the last filibuster of note, and ended the obsession to establish a racist nation in Nicaragua.

# 5

## "EL COLOSSO" INTERVENES

### *Destabilization & Dollar Diplomacy*

AFTER THE WALKER EPISODE, Central American attitudes toward the United States changed. No longer was America "the Great Republic of the North"; it was more practically termed "El Colosso," the intrusive colossus of North America. That diplomacy and business must be transacted with this calculating giant was inevitable, and profitable, but—look out!

At least the takeover filibusters were gone for good. The "immortals" lingered only in a crop of blue-eyed, blondish children around Rivas and other former Walker strongholds. In following years adventurous gringo handymen gradually took the places of soldiers of fortune. They operated the machines of modern technology as they seeped into the area. The peasants didn't understand machines or bookkeeping, and their social betters disdained to learn, even for supervisory positions. They did not wish to soil their hands or aristocratic reputations in an "occupation." The colorful misfits from America and Europe who operated commercial-industrial Latin America for more than fifty years were characterized thus by a resident journalist:

> *In the main these men were outcasts who could not go home—engineers who had run past switches or had taken one drink too many before getting into the cab, accountants who had failed to account, husbands who had accumulated more than the usual number of wives and been caught at it. For the most part they led drab and sordid lives and quickly or slowly, but always surely, drank themselves to death.*

They were the foot soldiers in a new type of American invasion, a commercial and corporate incursion more subtle than the filibusters'. As it expanded in Nicaragua it would draw in the U.S. government to such a degree that for twenty-five years El Colosso absolutely controlled the land.

For about thirty years after Walker, official American concerns for Nicaragua remained centered upon keeping out European influence and, futilely, negotiating and planning a Nicaraguan ocean-to-ocean transit ship canal. As in the past, great expectations for a canal came to nothing.

In 1881, a French company (guided by Ferdinand de Lesseps, who had masterminded the Suez Canal) began digging across the isthmus of Panama. A decade later, after a ghastly death toll from tropical disease and $200 million-plus spent, the project faltered. American surveys of both Panama and Nicaragua favored the latter. However, shifting political policy in these nations delayed and frustrated the project until, in 1902, President Theodore Roosevelt determined to activate the canal project as a national-defense necessity. In Congress the Nicaraguan option was presented in competition with the French Panamanian (whose company wished to recoup a bit of their loss by selling their completed work to the Americans). Lobbying on both sides was lavish and extreme.

Then a natural event again shifted Nicaragua's destiny. On May 8, 1902, Mount Pelée, a volcano on the Caribbean island of Martinique, massively erupted and killed 40,000 persons. There were several smoking volcanos within the western rim of Nicaragua where the canal was to be dug. Opponents pictured the expensive ditch filled with molten lava! And then a Panamian lobbyist produced a Nicaraguan postage stamp that showed a railroad train and a smoking volcano. Each U.S. Senator received one of these stamps along with lava-and-earthquake propaganda. Shortly afterward the Senate went for the Panama route.

For many years after the Walker embarrassment his discredited Liberal-party allies in Nicaragua remained out of power. During the Conservatives' happy "Thirty Years" of dominance between 1863 and 1893, their politicians traded political jobs smoothly without a slip. In Nicaragua this didn't mean domestic tranquility. No, there were various attempted revolutions, and foreign war, too. A Guatemalan caudillo, Justo Rufino Barrios, attempted to reunite the Central American republics under his heel, but the ambitious Liberal fell in battle (1885). In the ensuing lull Central American development picked up, even in Nicaragua, which owned the worst reputation for instability and therefore trailed in foreign investment.

Behind the façade of the unusual period of single-party dominance, politics in Nicaragua went on as usual, including, for example, the sham of democratic elections. An observer described the local process in the early nineties:

> *On the eve of the day announced for the polling, the alcalde (political magistrate) of one of the larger towns despatched a batch of messengers to three*

*hundred or so residents in the district, requiring
their presence on the morrow under penalty of a
heavy fine. On arriving next day, they are ushered
into the Cabildo (government building) where the
alcalde wishes them good morning and summons his
clerk, who hands each man a strip of paper neatly
folded up, pointing at the same time to a box and
adding: "Put it in there, please."*

*Naturally Mr. Elector does as he is requested, after
which another clerk registers his name and address,
the alcalde comes forward and shakes him by the
hand, and the next moment he is in the street asking
the first passer-by what it all means. Next morning
the official gazette solemnly announces that by an
overwhelming majority Mr. "So-and-so" has been
elected . . . and so the matter ends.*

From time to time the opposition leaders, denied their
chance at the polls, decided they had gathered enough
strength to overwhelm the government. A revolution would
be attempted. Most of the uprisings are one- or two-inning
affairs. The government seizes all means of transport and
communications, both sides issue a call to arms, and all parti-
sans turn soldier for a few days. Officers, promoted to colonel
based on their ability to contribute "donations," outnumber
ordinary (poor, lower-class) foot soldiers, who are forced into
service.

A sharp engagement or two, a little blood spilled, and
(one hopes), if all went well, it is obvious who is now on top.
"But the whole business is soon over; if the insurrectionary
party gets the advantage, the government instantly retires,
and so matters are arranged."

In 1893 the Conservatives mismanaged their succession,
and the successful revolution that followed produced

Nicaragua's first real caudillo, Jose Santos Zelaya, who ruled absolutely and spectacularly for sixteen years. A caudillo is a Latin American political leader who rises above his party (here Liberal) and creates a personal organization to sustain his power. Under Zelaya elections were more brazenly rigged than ever: El Presidente once amused himself by decreeing the presidential candidates to be Jose, Santos, and Zelaya: *Voters, please make your choice!*

Zelaya was of proud, wealthy, aristocratic origin; his family over centuries had kept their Castilian blood line pure, with no Indian mixture. He was extensively educated in Europe and returned determined upon a political career. He was well supplied with the ego, ambition, and ruthless cynicism necessary to become a Napoleon of Central America.

Zelaya, a Liberal, began political agitation in Nicaragua. He understood that the Conservative government would not long allow it, but the young man needed to make a reputation for the day when there would be a Liberal opportunity in Nicaragua. Because of his family's position Zelaya didn't have to worry about imprisonment—exile would be the punishment. And so it was. Foresightedly he attached himself to the Guatemalan caudillo Barrios, the better to study how to take over Central America. After his teacher unexpectedly was killed, Zelaya moved on to further political mastering in El Salvador before a Nicaraguan opportunity opened. He was forty when he took over his native land.

Zelaya has some admirers, for he was the first Nicaraguan leader who truly led. There was a good deal of internal improvement aided by foreign investment during his regime. And nationalistic citizens certainly applauded the independent way he acted on the international stage. Zelaya was his own man; he thumbed his nose at the USA when he felt like it. But the dictator also displayed two repellent aspects of *"caudillismo."*

He was cruel and ruthless in a cavalier fashion inside his nation. For example, the technique of the forced loan was often used: A landowner was asked to lend (give) money to the government. If he refused, perhaps a cache of arms would be planted on his property, be "discovered," and he jailed as an enemy and his lands taken altogether by the regime. Torture of political opponents featured a Zelaya specialty—the chili-pepper enema. Also, it was no joke to say: *Hide your daughters! El presidente is near!* Zelaya is said to have boasted fathering forty-five children.

And Zelaya used his power to line and stuff his pockets. His principal technique was to create monopolies of practically all commercial activity within the country. If permission was desired to, say, run a store, or sell produce, one saw Zelaya (specifically his son-in-law, who dispensed and collected) to secure and pay for the permit—and pay and pay. Similarly, American and European business interests paid to get operating concessions within Nicaragua. The concessions were issued helter-skelter. Some were valuable, others worthless or duplicates. They paid and took their chances. So, to be happy in Nicaragua between 1893 and 1909 it *paid* to be a Zelayaista.

According to some sources, the caudillo wished to depart in later years but was restrained by his subordinates, who realized that their source of graft would disappear if he went.

In matters of state, President Zelaya moved quickly to squash the lingering independence of the Mosquito Coast and bind the region firmly to the nation. Since this maneuver was anti-British, it had the approval of the United States. But in his foreign policy Zelaya scorned U.S. opinions. He was a mover and shaker of Central America and beyond, even becoming involved in revolution in distant Ecuador.

Between Zelaya and Guatemalan caudillo Cabrera lay weaker Honduras and El Salvador. Zelaya's efforts to take

over Honduras and destabilize El Salvador resulted in wars
with conservative factions. Cabrera took care to court U.S.
approval. Zelaya did not (his blind spot as a practical opera-
tor), and after the canal prize was awarded to Panama he
shed any pretense of pleasing Americans. So the Nicaraguan
strong man became identified in American opinion as the
Central American bully.

Two area peace conferences arranged through President Theodore Roosevelt's diplomacy failed to settle matters satisfactorily for the United States. Nicaragua and
America were on a collision course because the U.S. shifted
in the years of Zelaya's rule from being solely the aloof, pure
champion to an attitude of "preventing anyone from inter-
fering with the Latin Americans—except ourselves."

By the beginning of the twentieth century America was
a roaring industrial nation seeking raw materials and mar-
kets at home and overseas. In a short war the U.S. had
stripped Spain of its overseas possessions: It now owned the
Philippines and Puerto Rico and held a tight protectorate
over Cuba—and felt self-confident as a genuine world
power.

Theodore Roosevelt was the embodiment of that spirit
and as president from 1901 to 1908 added the "Roosevelt
corollary" to the Monroe Doctrine. Historian Wilfrid Call-
cott imagines T. R. describing it:

> *These are our younger brothers. When they need
> spanking we expect to do the job, and incidentally
> when we think it advisable we shall take charge of
> their spending money, and, maybe of certain other
> choice possessions in the meantime.*

Roosevelt fitted actions to words by fomenting revolution in
Colombia's province of Panama and got a better Canal deal
from an independent republic of Panama. Also the U.S. took

over the government's bookkeeping in the Dominican Republic when American investors faced losses. The Nicaraguan caudillo imprudently ignored these signs.

In 1908 the American ambassador to Nicaragua, John Gardner Coolidge, resigned his post in disgust. In Washington he told his superiors that Zelaya was "all to the bad" and that an overturn was desirable; a beginning would be the chilling of U.S. relations with the dictator. So the U.S. did not send a new ambassador to Managua, and Zelaya's enemies pricked up their attention.

The Taft administration, entering 1909, included a former corporation lawyer, Secretary of State Philander C. Knox, who brought a corporate outlook to the job. Knox had a plan to end instability in the Caribbean–Central American area; its buzz words were "dollar diplomacy." They were inspired by President Taft's speech in which he proposed to "substitute dollars for bullets," meaning that prosperity would smother the impulse to revolution.

The United States would pay off the republics' European debts with dollars and pump in new American money, *with the U.S.* overseeing the debtor nation's revenue sources to ensure repayment (and make money for U.S. investors). Dollar diplomacy appeared to be working in Cuba and the Dominican Republic, Knox believed, and he wished to spread the fiscal technique into Central America. There were plenty of dollars—U.S. wealth increased in the first twelve years of the twentieth century from $88 billion to $186 billion.

Zelaya ignored this, and in 1909 made all the wrong moves. Needing money, he ignored American sources and set about arranging a huge loan in Europe. And in his concessions game with outside corporations, Zelaya most inopportunely canceled the gold-mine franchise of the La Luz y Los Angeles Company, an American venture. Secretary of State Knox was a notable stockholder in La Luz. The caudillo also stirred dislike by failing to change a banana concession.

The pervasive United Fruit Company known to Latin Americans as *El Pulpo* (the octopus) had mostly bypassed volatile Nicaragua for Costa Rica, Panama, and Guatemala. But a tentacle of *El Pulpo* was the Bluefields Steamship Company, which bought bananas from mostly American independent growers in eastern Nicaragua and shipped them north. It held Zelaya's concession (monopoly) for this service.

In 1909, United Fruit abruptly depressed the price it would pay for Nicaraguan bananas to about 35 percent below what it paid in other countries. Zelaya did not respond to the plea of the independents for relief from the price-gouging monopoly practice. So there was a banana war that summer around Bluefields—night riders and plantation trashing as the independents strove to enforce an embargo rather than sell at ruinous rates. Anti-Zelaya feeling was intense.

A Conservative revolution, centering on Bluefields, started in the fall. Zelaya's resident governor, General Manuel Estrada, was lured into the revolution by being promised the presidency. The visible organizer of the revolt, however, and its banker, was a rather young and quiet man, Adolfo Diaz.

Diaz, of good family, had studied in the States and become a friend of America and American ways. He didn't mind having an occupation and worked in the office of that same La Luz y Los Angeles Company, the Knox-oriented American gold mine that Zelaya had molested. Though this clerk earned only about thirty-five dollars a week he was certainly a saver, for somehow (perhaps with U.S. aid), Diaz was able to bankroll the revolution with six hundred thousand dollars!

On October 10, General Estrada seized Bluefields on behalf of the revolution. The United States had been tipped beforehand and so was able to plan ahead. An east coast republic was proclaimed, and Estrada promised that the new regime intended to overwhelm the rest of Nicaragua.

Zelaya was used to revolts, having put down a dozen or so in sixteen years. He despatched an army toward Bluefields and soon four-thousand-plus government troops ranged outside the town. Estrada had only about five hundred soldiers. But he added the strongest ally when he told the American consul he had heard that Zelaya had instructed his troops to loot the town and be tough on Americans because they were at the bottom of the trouble. Handily, an American fleet had been stationed nearby and in short order four hundred U.S. Marines were landed at Bluefields to protect American lives and property . . . and the revolution.

Major Smedley D. Butler commanded the marines on this occasion. A marine's marine (two Congressional Medals of Honor), the plain-spoken future major general knew his role and played it well.

*It didn't take a ton of bricks to make me see daylight. It was plain that Washington would like the revolutionists to come out on top.*

*I wrote a letter to Lara and Godoy, the two government generals besieging the town, informing them that we were neutral and were on the scene merely to protect American residents. We had no objection to their taking Bluefields, if it could be managed without shooting. . . .*

Quoted excerpt is from *Old Gimlet Eye,* by Smedley Butler as told to Lowell Thomas, © 1933.

*"How are we to take the town if we can't shoot? And won't you also disarm the revolutionists defending the town?" the government generals wrote back to me.*

*"There is no danger of the defenders killing American citizens, because they will be shooting outwards," I replied suavely, "but your soldiers will be firing toward us."*

*The generals bombarded everybody of importance with letters of appeal, without gaining support for their position. Finally they sputtered out the Nicaraguan equivalant of "Oh, hell," and moved away.*

Thereby the infant revolution was saved from strangulation in its crib. And now President Zelaya made his last and most serious error. Two American soldiers of fortune, enlisted with Estrada's force, attempted to dynamite Nicaraguan government troop ships coming down the San Juan River. They were captured, held, and executed at Zelaya's order, though the U.S. representative in Managua had pleaded for their lives.

The victims were professional anti-Zelaya adventurers who had been detained during three other revolutionary attempts and released each time. Zelaya had his reasons for an end to patience. However, since the caudillo was a military midget beside "El Colosso," it was foolhardy to arouse the fury of the United States.

It was just the incident that Secretary of State Knox needed, and used, to sever U.S. relations with Nicaragua. He sent a scathing undiplomatic note personally attacking President Zelaya, judging him "a blot on the history" of his country; it was clear that the USA would never again negotiate with him. Checkmated and fearing an American invasion, the ex-strongman resigned in favor of vice-president Jose Madriz and left the country.

Madriz was a much more virtuous politician than Zelaya, but the American government was not impressed. They wanted a complete housecleaning. So they declared that pending the outcome of the revolution the United States would recognize neither faction. When Madriz's forces attempted to crush the revolt at its source in Bluefields, the Americans again interposed their naval units and allowed neither an attack nor a blockade of the port.

The evident destabilizing intention of awesome "El Colosso" wilted Nicaraguan confidence in the Madriz regime's future, and the resulting process of changing sides brought the Zelayaista government to collapse by October 1910. General Estrada moved into Managua, the new capital of Nicaragua established at the lakes link as a neutral site between conservative Granada and Liberal León. One of Estrada's first official actions as president was to cable warm regards to Secretary of State Knox.

Madriz was certainly honorable in that he left a goodly sum in the national treasury. The Conservatives dissipated it. Prominent revolutionists were paid off, and of course there were numerous claims of Conservatives wronged by Zelaya. The printing presses hummed and saturated Nicaragua with unbacked paper money, inducing a national financial crisis.

The new government was politically shaky. Other generals who had joined the revolt wanted to be president, especially General Luis Mena. President Estrada, risen from the lower class (an ex-carpenter), had inferiority feelings and feared his rival. El Presidente got drunk of an evening and bravely ordered General Mena arrested for treason. Sobering next morning, he panicked, resigned, and left the country that same day.

In 1911 Adolfo Diaz, one-time mining company clerk, was elevated to power. Well meaning, colorless, compliant, he was the man the Americans wanted all along. For the next dozen years he and others of his type would rule through fixed elections as a minority party. "The natural sentiment of an overwhelming majority of the Nicaraguans is antagonistic to the United States," reported the American ambassador from the new U.S. protectorate.

Nicaragua got a strong dose of Dollar Diplomacy. The State Department induced Wall Street bankers to lend millions. It was "safe" because the U.S. supervised the Nicaraguan customs houses and allowed the bankers to take over the national bank and the railroad. The country was tagged "The Brown Brothers' Republic" in a match of the brown-skinned natives with the name of the principal U.S. banking house.

This process had not been under way two years when the ambitious General Mena tired of waiting for the presidency and revolted. Diaz felt helpless and asked for American intervention. In came the U.S. Marines again, Major Smedley D. Butler commanding. Their mission was to secure the railroad, relieve the capital of rebel pressure, and follow through in ending the revolt. The four hundred marines were the key, the forward edge of victory, with the government troops happy to mop up and loot behind the Americans. Major Butler and his marines had their adventures, for example, a one-on-one confrontation with a rebel general on the track outside León:

   . . . *His black eyes flashed with rage. We stood facing each other. When he scowled, I grinned.*

   *"What's the use of wasting time?" I burst out. "I'm going on to Corinto. Now what are you going to do about it?"*

*Before I could wink an eye, he jerked his pistol out of his belt and shoved it into my midriff.*

*"If the train moves, I shoot."*

*One hundred red blooded Americans were clustered around the locomotive at the other end of the bridge, watching tensely to see what I would do. I couldn't retreat and lose face. If I signaled to the Marines to shoot, there would be a frightful slaughter. I had to act quickly. I made a grab for the General's gun and had the luck to tear it out of his hand. A bit theatrical I emptied the cartridges out of the barrel. His army burst out laughing. They could appreciate a joke even when it was on them.*

Butler and company penetrated into Granada, negotiated with the seriously ill General Mena, talked him into giving up and leaving Nicaragua. On the way back to Managua the Americans assaulted and captured two stubborn rebel hilltop strongholds and ended the revolt. Six marines were killed in the campaign. About a thousand Nicaraguans on both sides died in the revolt.

Major Butler and most of his tough hombres sailed away, but from 1912 to 1925 a "Legation Guard" of one hundred marines remained in Nicaragua. They kept the peace. A few abrasive incidents with the populace were quickly and fairly handled with stiff penalties to guilty marines. An incidental gift from the guard was Yankee baseball, which the natives took up with enthusiasm. The marines tried, as often as possible, to umpire local contests. In true Nicaraguan fashion the losers could not abide losing. There were brawls, knife fights, murders, between opposing teams.

In 1916, the USA and Nicaragua settled the Canal matter when the U.S. agreed to pay Nicaragua $3 million for all rights over ninety-nine years. No European competitor for the Panama Canal could ever enter here. For the Nicaraguans, years passed in peaceful bondage. In 1919, Zelaya died in relative poverty in his apartment on upper Broadway in New York City. His European-invested fortune had been largely wiped out during World War I. He had spent most of his lonely exile in America, which seems a strange choice.

Dollar diplomacy rectified Nicaraguan finances, but slowly. Respectable profits (about 15 percent) were earned by the bankers; the country was not gouged. There was a lot of American do-it-our-way paternalistic advice and aid in political, economic, and hygenic affairs, which was docilely accepted, and sometimes discarded as soon as Yankee attention shifted elsewhere.

By 1924, tiring of unceasing Latin American and world disapproval, the U.S. dared to arrange a marginally fair election and promised to withdraw somewhat. The election winners, a potentially unstable Conservative/Liberal combination, seemed willing to go on with the United States. But again there was an ambitious general awaiting his chance.

On August 3, 1925, with colors flying and band blaring, the U.S. Marine detachment marched to the station as some bystanders hissed and some cheered. Longtime girlfriends tossed kisses and called *"Adios, Marinos!"*

But not for very long!

# 6

# THE MARINES MEET
# GENERAL SANDINO
## *A Patriot Folk Hero*
## *Outlasts the USA*

AS THE MOST visible American presence sailed away
from Nicaragua, the U.S. State Department hoped that the
made-in-America political structure they had left behind
would be a prize example of sturdy endurance. But it turned
out to be a house of cards that began to blow away at the first
determined revolutionary puff, only three weeks after the
marines departed.

Conservative General Emiliano Chamorro Vargas was
a loser in the 1924 election. He was sore because all the votes
from his home area had been thrown out by political opponents in power. Chamorro didn't want to wait four years and
then perhaps face a rigged election. He viewed the elected
president, fellow Conservative Carlos Solorzano, as a push-
over politician without the clout or stomach for a brawl, and
so he decided to push.

On the evening of August 28, a top-level government
reception was going on at Managua's International Club.

81

President Solorzano had left, but the cream of society and government remained, as did the American ambassador Charles Eberhardt. Abruptly the party was crashed by "a threatening coatless figure in boots, spurs and military breeches, with a broad-brimmed hat pulled well down over his face, flourishing a revolver in each hand" and leading a pack of ruffians. He was Gabry Rivas, brother of General Alfredo Rivas, the current Nicaraguan military chieftain. He staggered drunkenly to the center of the dance floor and roared out that he had come to rescue the president from the clutches of his Liberal cabinet ministers!

Rivas highlighted his B-movie villain image by pointing his pistols haphazardly toward the ceiling and blazing away. He captured the attention of all present! Ladies screamed and fainted; the space beneath the billiard tables in the game room became layered with panicky gentlemen. The targeted Liberal politicians arose in varied states of decorum. Punctuated by volleys of show-off revolver shooting, the scene lasted nearly an hour until the Rivas gang had detected all the victims on their list. The invaders did not fear police interference.

The American ambassador became clustered about with hopeful refugees seeking protection. Wives pleaded for intercession on behalf of captured husbands. But all that Eberhardt could do was maintain his cool.

As the captives were pushed toward the exit it was a moment of truth: Would they be lined up against the nearest wall and executed? Reaction varied. Liberal cabinet member General Jose Maria Moncada, with a pistol probing his paunch, snarled: "You coward!" But another official briefly broke away from his guard and:

*flung himself at the feet of the American Minister.*
*As his captors dragged him away he threw his arms*
*around the Minister's waist, and, his head under the*

*tails of the the Minister's evening coat, begged the
protection of the United States. It was this incident,
probably, which caused the report that he had
draped himself in the American flag to claim
asylum.*

The hostages were hustled up to La Loma, the fortress
overlooking Managua captained by General Rivas, and imprisoned until the weakling president signed an order firing
his Liberal officials. Liberal Vice-President Juan Bautista
Sacasa prudently retreated to his home in Liberal territory
at León. General Chamorro, the slightly concealed hand
behind it all, now came into the capital to overawe President Solorzano. He did not violently overthrow the helpless
government. By strong-arm threats he privately obtained
the president's resignation in writing and pocketed it for
future use as necessary. By semilegal maneuvering he
worked his way into the "vacant" vice-presidency. In late
January 1926 President Solorzano, "for reasons of health,"
resigned and Chamorro took over.

This delicate, for Nicaragua, political dance had been
staged to smooth approval of the succession by the United
States. But the State Department, aware of every crooked
step, refused to accept Chamorro and stuck to its refusal.
U.S. foreign-policy officials were smarting under intense foreign criticism of imperialism in Latin America. They had
dressed up Nicaragua with an approximation of a working
American democracy and now Chamorro had messed it all
up. So they left him dangling without U.S. recognition and
awaited his eventual fall. Interested parties noted a power
vacuum in the land.

In the meantime former vice-president Sacasa exited
the country just ahead of a hit squad. Officials in Washington
were nice but didn't help him. The State Department dis-
trusted Liberal Nicaraguan aims. Sacasa went on and found

material aid and comfort in Mexico. Soon he, with an army and Mexican supply line, had established a Liberal beachhead in northeast Nicaragua and revolutionary war again convulsed the nation.

Now Washington's Nicaragua experts had a distressful headache because they were anxious about a possible "bolshevik" Mexico. A somewhat socialistic, very nationalistic revolution in Mexico had recently discomfited the substantial U.S. business interests there. War had even been considered. Was Sacasa the figurehead for a Mexican-controlled Communist Nicaragua? One might easily imagine the finger-shaking ghost of Teddy Roosevelt crying: *Protect the Canal!* But on the Conservative side all they had was the publicly discarded Chamorro. So the policy makers reached for the U.S. Marines.

Using the well-worn plea of "protecting American lives and property," hundreds of marines and special navy Bluejackets were landed in the latter months of 1926 and early 1927. They established several "neutral zones," where revolutionary activity was suppressed, and generally hoped that their so-called neutral presence would aid the government in power at Managua.

Chamorro had finally vacated the presidency (and been awarded the plush ambassadorship in Washington), while the good old, reliable U.S. patsy, Adolfo Diaz, was again in the president's chair. But the war, beyond ruining the always precarious national finances, was going against the central government. It seemed that the more intervention, the more popular the revolution! General Moncada, hassled and imprisoned by the Rivas gang a year past, was winning Liberal victories (more now for himself than for party leader Sacasa) and was moving patiently toward Managua and triumph.

But the American president, Calvin Coolidge, was not about to give up on U.S. influence in Latin America. He selected a crack negotiator, Henry L. Stimson, and sent him south with a new approach and a tough warning.

General Moncada was very near Managua when the crucial meeting occurred under a thorn tree beside the Tipitapa River, a shady spot in no-man's-land between the ragged armies. The U.S., Stimson said, was dead serious about three requirements in absolutely ending the conflict: (1) The present regime must survive; (2) U.S. Marines would completely disarm both armies, thereby stopping the war; (3) The United States promised to oversee and enforce a *completely fair* election in 1928. Presidential candidates, Conservative and Liberal, were invited and would campaign freely.

The Sacasa-Moncada Liberals were not nationalistic anti-Americans at all. Generally they wanted to nudge aside the Conservatives and take their place at the U.S. feed trough in Managua. So Moncada was inclined to go along with points two and three, but balked at allowing Diaz another year and a half, at least, in the presidency.

Stimson, a former army colonel, stared down the Liberal general as he played his trump card. How would he, General Moncada, like to fight the U.S. Marines? No, Moncada replied, he would not. He respectfully asked Stimson to put the American plan and the consequences of bucking it into writing so that he could show it to his lesser generals. It was done, and the complete Stimson plan was agreed to by all but one insignificant Liberal general. Stimson was proud to have fitted an American peace upon Nicaragua. The war was over, he said, except perhaps for a bit of skirmishing with persons who were "bandits," not legitimate soldiers.

The disarmament proceeded splendidly, for President Diaz authorized a bounty payment of ten dollars per firearm from either army, quite a personal bonanza. Thousands of rifles and over three hundred machine guns were collected by the Marines, who now exercised all police and military functions in the land until the National Guard (the Guardia), in training by U.S. instructors, could be relied on. There was universal joy as the discharged troops returned to their families in time to plant the spring crops. It seemed a slight problem that Moncada's dissenting general had refused to disarm his small band and had withdrawn into a rugged natural fortress of jumbled mountains and jungle in the northwest near the Honduran border.

The U.S. officials discounted General Augusto Cesar Sandino as a bandit-type fighter who didn't want to give up living off the land. General Moncada, who had disliked Sandino strongly enough to try by tactical fiddling to get him killed in battle, bad-mouthed the rebel as an upstart leading a small rabble.

A reinforced marine patrol was sent up and stationed in Ocotal, the town nearest to the "bandit" lair. The marines were restrained. They were to observe and wait until Sandino tired of swatting mosquitos in the jungle and came in and surrendered arms. But General Sandino seemed to be popular in the bush, and he sounded more like a patriot than a bandit: "I will die with the few that follow me because it is preferable to die as rebels by fire and sword than to live as slaves."

That statement was for public relations. In the dialogue of messages he established with Captain G. D. Hatfield, U.S. Marines, Ocotal, he sounded more earthy and banditlike. Sandino ferociously dared the American officer to come out to single combat, promised Hatfield and his unit grisly deaths, and in a lighter mood told the captain that he wished to put him "in a handsome tomb with flowers." Hatfield's reply to this paper barrage was: "If words were men and horses phrases, you'd be a field marshal instead of a mule thief."

After Sandino's force attacked, stripped, and blew up an

American-owned mine, U.S. headquarters altered their go-slow policy: Give him a last-chance ultimatum before we squash them. Captain Hatfield duly messaged: *Come in and surrender, or we will go out and disarm you.* There was no saucy or threatening paper response. One hour after the mid-July deadline, in the stealth of tropic night, the general and at least three hundred of his "Sandinista" followers came down from the mountains to kill the Americans at Ocotal.

There were thirty-eight Marines and forty-nine Guardias within a fortified complex of armory and barrack in Ocotal, all asleep save a single sentry. Sandino's planned 1 A.M. massacre was a near thing. But with the timely alarm of the vigilant sentry, men sprang from their beds, seized weapons, and repelled the initial attack. Meanwhile a Sandinista squad covertly climbed over a back wall and penetrated the fortress. Their movement within was heard by Captain Hatfield through a wall. He leaped into the room and wiped out the invaders with a blazing revolver volley. A second general attack in the dark hours was also repulsed.

In the morning daylight, General Sandino, who had directed the operation from a hilltop outside of Ocotal, sent in messengers demanding submission. Hatfield's reply was elemental: Marines do not surrender. A drone swelled in the sky as the marine morning air patrol approached. A message had been laid out in the barrack's courtyard: "Am being attacked by Sandino. One dead, several wounded, need assistance." Meanwhile one of the two planes landed routinely outside of town. It was warned away by natives and took off amid a hail of Sandinista lead.

After strafing the enemy, the planes hurried back to Managua's airfield. Soon five brand-new marine dive bombers arrived over Ocotal and began a machine-gun stitchery upon Sandino's troops. Each plane carried a gunner-observer; the targeted enemy was riddled both coming and going, while seventeen-pound shrapnel bombs were tossed toward troop concentrations. For forty-five minutes they repeatedly swept in on low-level strafing passes. Unassisted they broke the will of the Sandinistas, hustled them into retreat and soon to disorderly rout. This type of air attack had not been done for real before. On July 16, 1927, the Vought Corsair airplane was king of the hill at Ocotal!

General Sandino left forty dead in Ocotal and suffered many hidden casualties in the retreat, perhaps up to one-third of his army. But this double disaster to manpower and his generalship did not disturb his popular rule in the back country. Additionally, Sandino exhibited adaptability. Not again would he engage the marines in head-on battle. The Sandinistas became skilled in the guerrilla arts: Strike for forage and destruction where the foe is absent or weak, and do not attack an enemy force except from ambush advantage.

"Am being attacked by Sandino . . . need assistance." This marine plea for help against a "bandit" with three hundred men alerted the media and focused U.S. and world attention on the Ocotal affair and the man who provoked it. Some bandit! Who was he anyway?

Augusto Sandino Calderon was born May 19, 1893, in the village of Niquinohomo near Masaya in central western Nicaragua. He was the "natural" (illegitimate) child of coffee planter Gregorio Sandino and servant woman Margarita Calderon. His father favored him and saw to it that he received some education. Young Sandino had a knack for mechanics and in his travels would support himself as an itinerant repairman.

A short-fused temper started him on his travels at age twenty-five after he shot a hometown official. In Honduras the refugee got into a brawl, with the result that he was declared an undesirable alien and had to move on. For five years he wandered in El Salvador, Guatemala, then Mexico, where in 1925 he appears on record as a warehouseman with an American oil company at Tampico.

When the Liberal revolution-invasion began in Nicaragua the following year, Sandino, who became politicized in Mexico, followed into their safe area in the northeast and found a job as timekeeper at an American-owned mine. Here he began effective sociopolitical haranguing of mine workers and peasants in the area. In Mexico he had become imbued with modern ideas about labor rights: the eight-hour day, negotiated wages and benefits. Beyond such local issues, he also emphasized the overall exploitation of the poor by the rich and expounded his hatred for the Yankee invaders who protected the wealthy. So he was attracted to the Liberals' revolutionary war and, having gathered a few dozen followers, approached the Liberal military chieftain Moncada to be enlisted as a "general."

General Sandino had a hard time getting started. He had to scrounge for his armament and beg to be allowed to campaign cohesively with General Moncada, who ignored, disdained, and came to strongly dislike this sloganeering, independent-minded subordinate. Sandino became convinced that Moncada wouldn't be much of an improvement over President Diaz and saw his impression confirmed when the commanding general cut his deal with the Americans. Moncada was a traitor! Well, if there were no patriots among Nicaragua's craven "leaders," then he, now Augusto *Cesar* Sandino, would maintain in the mountains the pure flame of Nicaraguan nationalism!

After Ocotal, for the rest of 1927 and indeed through all of 1928, the U.S. Marines attempted to enforce their periodic promises that extermination of "the bandits" was at hand. Strong marine patrols on muleback bearing a machine gun or two probed doggedly if blindly into Sandino country. And it was *his* turf: The Sandinistas always knew exactly where the marines were plodding, shadowed them, even photographed the patrols, and sometimes provided treacherous guides to marine officers confused in the jumbled terrain. The far-seeing marine eyes were the air patrols. But jungle cover hampered guerrilla detection, and later strafing actions were not as productive as at Ocotal (the planes were banned from attacking troop concentrations in residential areas unless fired upon).

The patrols trudged vigilantly, for they knew that at the end of the trail would be an ambush if there was to be any fighting at all. The marines learned to cope very well in the ambushes, to immediately deploy and directly attack the weakest enemy flank under their machine-gun coverage. Though the guerrillas did a lot of shooting, they failed remarkably in inflicting marine casualties. On only a handful of well-publicized occasions over years did they heavily damage a marine patrol.

In the attempt to contain and liquidate the Sandinista force the marine presence swelled to 5,700 men. General Sandino probably amassed no more than 2,500 guerrillas. But the U.S. couldn't catch Sandino. When the marines thought he was penned in some mountain fastness, the slippery general would appear raiding east or southwest, maybe hundreds of miles away. Very frustrating, and embarrassing!

In addition to his guerrilla skills, Sandino possessed a fine talent for public relations. He postured as the hero underdog, a kind of Nicaraguan Robin Hood. All Latin America was inspired, and thrilled to his patriot stand against the intrusive El Colosso. A noisy minority within the United States also applauded General Sandino.

Public ridicule of Sandino's "bandit" title was widespread, but the State Department clung to it. The U.S. was in Nicaragua to help the locals to help themselves. If political status, even a negative one, was awarded to Sandino, the United States' position would become even more painful internationally. The Americans would be seen as nakedly fighting *against Nicaraguans.* U.S. foreign-policy stylists squirmed and portrayed Sandino as a communist bandit.

This seems to be untrue. The Communists of course embraced Sandino as a revolutionary personality (military units were named for him). But Augusto Cesar was no hombre to follow the party line. His half-formed social impulses appear populistic; he was one-dimensional, a patriot folk hero: Kill, drive the Americans out of Nicaragua, and overturn their stooges! The Communists gave up on the general and ended by publicly denouncing him.

Sandino's most important public-relations triumph in the United States was a result of an interview given to a swashbuckling American foreign correspondent, Carleton Beals, at the beginning of 1928. It would have been suicidal for most U.S. reporters to seek out Sandino, but Beals had a fondness for military-political Latin American underdogs, and it was known to Sandino that he was on assignment from *The Nation,* an American journal pledged to getting the United States out of Nicaragua. So Sandino welcomed the Yankee correspondent and comported himself in his best charismatic style. Beals was enthralled:

> *He is short, not more than five feet five. When I saw him he was dressed in a uniform of dark-brown with almost black puttees, immaculately polished; a silk red-and-black handkerchief knotted about his throat; and a broad-brimmed Texas Stetson hat, pulled low over his forehead and pinched shovel-shaped. Occasionally, as we conversed, he shoved his sombrero to the back of his head and hitched his chair forward. The gesture revealed straight black hair and a full forehead. His face makes a straight line from the temple to the jaw-bone. His jaw-bone makes a sharp angle with the rest of his face, slanting to an even, firm jaw. His regular, curved*

*eyebrows are arched high above liquid black eyes
without visible pupils. His eyes are of remarkable
mobility and refraction to light—quick, intense eyes.
He is utterly without vices, has an unequivocal sense
of personal justice and a keen eye for the welfare of
the humblest soldier. "Many battles have made our
hearts hard, but our souls are strong" is one of his
pet sayings. I am not sure of the first part of the
epigram, for in all the soldiers and all of the officers
I talked to he has stimulated a fierce affection and a
blind loyalty and has instilled his own burning
hatred of the invader.*

*"Death is but a tiny moment of discomfort not to be
taken seriously," he repeats over and over to his
soldiers. . . .*

Was Sandino "utterly without vices"? In personal relations and hygiene perhaps, but not in safeguarding elemental human rights. Nicaraguans and Americans captured during Sandinista operations were absolutely fortunate if they met death as "a tiny moment of discomfort." The machete ritual death was prevalent among the Sandinistas and evidence has been recorded that it was approved by General Sandino. This excruciating, diabolically slowed death was performed by slicing the limbs by portions and slashing the abdomen, ending with slicing off the top of the skull. The official Sandinista emblem featured the beheading of a U.S. Marine, and gross disfigurement of battlefield corpses by the guerrillas was common. Beals specifically questioned the general about this savagery. Sandino replied that it was an ancient Indian custom in the area. If Americans found the practice indelicate, they should stay out of his mountains and return to the USA.

Sandino was most eloquent when speaking on the sub-

ject of the pervasive U.S. presence in his homeland. He told
Beals:

> *We have taken up arms from love of our country*
> *because all other leaders have betrayed it and have*
> *sold themselves out to the foreigner or have bent the*
> *neck in cowardice. We, in our own house, are*
> *fighting for our inalienable rights. What right have*
> *foreign troops to call us outlaws and bandits and to*
> *say that we are the aggressors? I repeat that we are*
> *in our own house. We declare that we will never live*
> *in cowardly peace under a government installed by a*
> *foreign Power. Is this patriotism or is it not? And*
> *when the invader is vanquished, as some day he*
> *must be, my men will be content with their plots of*
> *ground, their tools, their mules, and their families.*

Within the United States similar pleas were made, including this gist of a Quaker telegram to President Coolidge:

> *Irrespective of whether you think that Sandino is a*
> *bandit or a patriot or both, it is undeniable that he*
> *is a Nicaraguan fighting on his own soil. . . . The*
> *United States will not make peace by shedding*
> *Nicaraguan blood. Do not exterminate Sandino.*

The Communist-backed All-American Anti-Imperialist
League featured Socrates Sandino, half-brother of the general, at mass rallies in New York City. They picketed at the
White House, bearing signs like WALL STREET AND NOT
SANDINO IS THE REAL BANDIT. Police arrested one hundred
seven protesters at that time. The League also issued "Sandino stamps" to paste on letters in addition to U.S. postage.

But the State Department was not going to allow its
prized U.S.–supervised, honest Nicaraguan election to be

canceled. In 1928 the tempo of the Sandino war increased. As humorist Will Rogers mused: The marines "are doing all they can to see that there are fewer votes to supervise and Sandino is doing all he can to see that there are fewer marines to supervise."

Marine aerial eyes finally discovered the celebrated El Chipote, Sandino's mountaintop fortress. A major expeditionary force struggled through the almost impassable jungle terrain to take the stronghold. When the marines at length assaulted it, they found no one but sombrero-topped straw men at the barricades. However, several ridges and valleys away, where Sandino and company really were, the fighting had been fierce and costly.

A riddled marine unit was besieged in the village of Quilili. They had eighteen wounded, some of whom would soon die without professional medical attention, and there was no prospect of overland relief for days to come. The ever vigilant air patrol was messaged the necessity of air evacuation as the marines tore down houses along the main village street to widen it and ready a nearly impossible "runway" out of a deeply rutted wagon road.

Skilled, quiet and unassuming, Lieutenant C. Frank Schilt volunteered to fly the missions. Somewhat protected by a strafing wingman, under fire from encircling Sandinistas each time, Schilt in his sturdy little Vought Corsair biplane swooped, bounced, swerved, skidded over the humpy surface, and successfully carried out the wounded and ferried in fourteen hundred pounds of supplies. What suspense must have gathered during ten trips in three days as he watched his plane shaking loose at the seams from the unreasonable thumpings and scrapings in landings and take-offs! Lieutenant Schilt was awarded the Congressional Medal of Honor and stayed on to become a general, commanding Marine aviation in Guadalcanal and elsewhere during World War II. Sandinista propaganda to the world portrayed the destruction of buildings at Quilili as a major American atrocity.

The marines and the expanding native Guardia did not catch General Sandino in 1928, but they contained him so that the Sandinistas did not interfere with the Nicaraguan presidential election. It proceeded splendidly, with a pair of marines overseeing each polling place as the Liberal General Moncada won handily. In the USA there was also a presidential election. Though the Democrats vowed to get out of Nicaragua, U.S. voters were more attracted to the Republican promise of four more years of prosperity and elected Herbert Hoover.

In 1929 Augusto Cesar Sandino attempted to collect personal and material dividends from all the Latin American and world liberal adulation he had stirred up. He selected Mexico as his host nation and spent most of the year there. But Mexican-American relations had improved to a point where Mexico asked for U.S. guidance regarding their standard of hospitality to Sandino. It was mutually agreed to ban his residence in the capital, so the guerrilla hero spent most of his stay in provincial Mérida, Yucatán, far from Mexico City. Sandino's dreams of international leadership and alliance remained dreams. He returned to the old routine in his mountains along the handy Honduran boundary, again stepping up guerrilla raiding in 1930 and thereafter. In a letter written in January 1931, Sandino made the dead-end observation that: "In order to save Nicaragua it is necessary to destroy it."

Under the Hoover administration the U.S. lost its proprietary zeal for intervention in Nicaragua. The terrible economic mess of the Great Depression strained at governmental attention and fibers. Anyway, had not the United States at great national cost installed a made-in-America democratic apparatus and forced it to work? It was in place—let the Nicaraguans carry on, and deal with Sandino, too!

Lawrence Dennis, formerly a diplomat on the front line of U.S. activities in Managua, described the new thinking when he wearily wrote in 1931:

> . . . *Nicaragua today furnishes the spectacle of a country spiritually and economically stagnant while to its illiterate and undernourished masses American marines vouchsafe that ultimate luxury of an advanced democracy—fair elections. One may even question whether the leader best suited to the needs of a country is likely to emerge from elections supervised by American officials as from a less artificial course of events.*
>
> *It is no disparagement of fair elections or the pax americana in Nicaragua to question whether these boons, by themselves, are worth to Nicaragua the life of one good American soldier. . . .*

Expansion and training of La Guardia Nacional, the Nicaraguan National Guard, became a top priority. A young man with a future, Anastasio Somoza, was in charge of the Guardia. This early exemplar of "a nice smile and iron teeth" knew how to get on with Americans (also Nicaraguans: He married a niece of President Sacasa). Somoza first appeared as an ingratiating interpreter during the Stimson mission. And he was a good dancer, too, according to the wife of the American ambassador. Yes, the Americans early on felt that they could get along with Somoza.

A spurt in U.S. casualties linked with Sandino's renewed incursions prompted greater U.S. desire to push the Guardia forward and pull back (and out of Nicaragua) marines whenever they could be replaced. The same Henry L. Stimson who in the intervention's palmy days had threatened to fight all of Moncada's army now announced, as Hoover's secretary of state, that the safety of U.S. citizens and property *could not* be guaranteed except in population centers where the shrunken marine force was now concentrated.

In 1932, Americans again supervised the Nicaraguan election, which Juan Sacasa, the Liberal politician previously shunted aside by General Moncada, now won as president. In the United States, Franklin D. Roosevelt was elected and proposed his new "Good Neighbor" policy to Latin America. Dollar diplomacy and intervention were obsolete doctrines. The U.S. Marines would be out of Nicaragua on January 1, 1933! Nicaraguan handling of the Sandino war appeared satisfactory under Somoza, who was coming on strong as a focus of political power. In any case—Nicaragua for Nicaraguans!

General Augusto Cesar Sandino had once predicted that "more than a battalion of your blond invaders will have bitten the dust of my wild mountains" in defeat. He settled for one hundred thirty-six marine casualties over six years. Now he fulfilled his vow that he fought only a foreign occupation. A month after the American withdrawal he signed in with President Sacasa as a normal political faction within the nation.

But tranquility did not favor Nicaragua. The political cage there was now uneasily crowded by three antagonistic species: a tiger (Somoza), a mountain lion (Sandino), and the pussycat (Sacasa) who glanced nervously at each of the other two in turn and wondered which of the beasts to ally himself with.

Henry L. Stimson: Diplomatic architect of the second Marine occupation, who was foiled as peacemaker by General Sandino.

Emiliano Chamorro was a U.S. friend and president of Nicaragua, but he was insufficiently "democratic" for official U.S. favor.

*General Sandino (center). Persistently termed "a bandit" by the U.S. government, he was a patriot-folk hero to many Latin Americans.*

*A typical Sandinista unit in their mountain camp.*

*The Guardia: General Somoza's muscle.*

A U.S. Marine unit en route in rural Nicaragua.

*Carleton Beals was the American journalist who popularized General Sandino in the U.S. press.*

*Lieutenant Christian F. Schilt was awarded the Congressional Medal of Honor for Marine rescue flights at Quilili.*

*General Moncada poses with Lieutenant Boyden, reputed to be the unfortunate decapitation victim depicted on the Sandinista seal.*

*The Sandinista national emblem.*

*Juan Sacasa: the president as "Pussy Cat."*

*Arthur Bliss Lane, U.S. ambassador to Nicaragua, was the man-in-the-middle at the time of Sandino's murder by the* Guardia.

*Anastacio Somoza: The man who knew how to talk to the Americans.*

# 7

# THE SOMOZA SUCCESSION

## *Liberty Is a "Hot Tamale"*

WHEN in February 1933 General Augusto Cesar Sandino agreed to peaceful relations with President Juan Sacasa's central government at Managua, he was entering upon the last year of his life, a time when his political naiveté led him finally to a firing squad. The pact that Sandino made with Sacasa was dignified and supportive of the former's independent stance—total amnesty for the Sandinistas, with government-financed settlement on an agricultural commune in the northeast and a limited reduction of their weaponry. Sandino remained an independent power within the nation, but he was not adept at the treacherous politics that were to follow.

Peace was an illusion. The newly powerful Guardia veterans hated Sandino. For years they had fought the dirtiest kind of no-quarter-given guerrilla warfare with the Sandinistas, and in recent years, as the marines eased out of the combat zones, had absorbed the brunt of ambush casualties, prisoner torture-death, and desecration. They believed, as the military often do in a stalemate, that with just a little more time and troops they would have avenged themselves upon the Sandinistas, perhaps in a massacre-style victory. Sacasa had sold them short!

These passions within the Guardia energized the conduct of General Anastasio Somoza, the Guardia commander. Somoza was no jungle fighter; he excelled as a realistic political planner, the crafty overseer of the Guardia's expansion to an overawing military presence in the land. Fantastic that the Americans had believed such a blunt instrument could be "nonpolitical"! Somoza intended the Guardia to be his strong springboard into the presidency—soon.

A few blocks away, in the presidential palace, sat jittery Juan Sacasa. He had a good network of political connections within the country, but was very short on military clout, barely able to raise a palace guard. Therefore, he made his opening to Sandino, the only available military force besides the Guardia. He understood Somoza's ambition but wanted to hang on in the presidency, in part because he was a henpecked statesman, and Juan Sacasa always strained to please Señora Sacasa. What should he do? Maybe the Americans would help; they should—the Nicaragua of today was their handiwork.

So when the new American ambassador, Arthur Bliss Lane, arrived, he was as popular as his recent predecessors had been. This was Lane's first ambassadorship and he wanted to make his mark. But Managua had become a U.S. diplomat's black hole, for America had lost interest in and developed an aversion to Nicaraguan politics. The envoy's instructions may be summarized as: Maintain the status quo, but do not expect *any* assistance from Washington. All that Lane got out of this assignment was frustration and a bum rap as an assassin's associate.

The styles of the supplicants to the ambassador matched their needs. Sacasa came out of weakness. He clutched at the hope of an American guarantee of his presidential tenure. Lane expressed his good wishes and did all that talking could accomplish, but offered no hope ever of a protective U.S. intervention. Somoza approached the envoy from a position of strength. He wanted only Lane's implicit consent to accept whatever Somoza might politically accomplish on his own. But he didn't get it, for the ambassador said he liked the status quo. The next election, Lane reminded Somoza, was not until 1936.

In the north, Augusto Cesar Sandino pondered his future. Sandino believed he had several choices. He could settle down here on the farm as a cautiously militant guardian and venerated folk hero. Or he might go abroad to take advantage of his popularity in an international leadership role. Perhaps he could magnetize that elusive union of the Central American nations, or maybe there was even a hemispheric role for General Sandino out there. But after months of ambivalence he decided to intensify his political role within Nicaragua, the most dangerous of the options. He struck out verbally at the Guardia, calling it unconstitutional, a remnant of U.S. rule. As the year closed, Sacasa was edging toward an alliance with Sandino. Without U.S. protection the nervous president thought it was his best chance to hang on against Somoza and the Guardia.

The renewed activity of General Sandino infuriated the Guardia. Then, in December, President Sacasa announced a plan to withdraw the Guardia from the northern Sandino country and allow the Sandinistas to administer police functions. The second stage of their weaponry reduction would be passed over. Then Sacasa dared to attempt to undercut the independent stance of the Guardia through reorganization. When these intentions were announced, General Somoza went around to tell both the president and the ambassador that he could not be held responsible for what the turbulent Guardia might goad itself into doing in this deplorable circumstance. It was a true warning.

When General Sandino looked toward Managua he was

power blind. He had a naive trust in the ability of President Sacasa to rule in his own capital. On two occasions Sandino had journeyed there to confer with the president and had arrived practically alone and unguarded. When the Guardia knew that he was coming again, to endorse Sacasa's latest overtures, they conspired to kill him.

Anastasio ("Tacho") Somoza Garcia spent a lot of time making up to Ambassador Lane. Americans had always been important to Somoza, and U.S. attitudes would be the keystone of his political future. Tacho, born in 1896, was the son of a respectable coffee planter, but he proudly counted Bernabe Somoza (hanged 1849) among his forebearers. Bernabe, widely known as *Siete Pañuelos* ("Seven Handkerchiefs," to mop his bloody hands), was the most notorious bandit of that era. His grandnephew would show him up!

When Tacho was nineteen he impregnated a house servant and was packed off to live with a relative in Philadelphia, Pennsylvania, and get some practical business schooling. He quickly adapted to Stateside living, and more importantly for his future, absorbed the popular culture and its dialogue. He could talk to an American like an American, especially at the common or coarse level. Also in Philly he met Salvadora ("Yoya") Debayle. Somoza would woo her, in love with her beauty and charm, her family relations (the Sacasas), and the connections within the Nicaraguan upper class that could be squeezed from all that. The ardent young suitor followed her back to León, overcame with charm the objections of her physician father, and the couple had a grand wedding and honeymoon.

Money was scarce as the bridegroom hopped from one job or promotion to another. He sold cars, introduced boxing to Nicaragua, read meters, and inspected outhouses. He and a friend conspired and counterfeited currency. Tacho was found out, but his connections kept him out of jail. When the 1926 revolution approached his area, Somoza gathered neighbors and for Moncada's Liberals captured his hometown bloodlessly but temporarily. The new "general" was soon captured. One of his captors recognized him (those good old family connections), gave him some money, and told him to get lost before he got hurt. Tacho went to Costa Rica for a few months, but cleverly reappeared at Moncada's elbow at the time of the Stimson negotiations, there beginning his climb through self-ingratiation to the Americans and then having the political savvy to sense the importance of the opportunity for an administrative role in the new Guardia.

Now General Somoza repeatedly talked to Ambassador Lane about Sandino. He expected sympathy, for hadn't the Americans fought the general through years of frustration? And now the fellow was stirring up new troubles. Surely the minister understood his problem, our problem . . . He repeated at their last meeting on the subject his desire to "lock Sandino up" and thereby solve everything. Tacho confidently asked Lane "to wink his eye" and the Guardia would take care of it. But Lane replied that "it" would be a rash action and compelled Somoza to promise to do nothing without further consideration and consultation.

On the evening of February 21, 1934, General Sandino attended a dinner at President Sacasa's palace. Their negotiations had progressed and it was a congenial occasion. Afterward, at about ten-thirty, the automobile carrying Sandino, two aides, his father, and a Sacasa cabinet minister who was Sandino's host was halted by a Guardia unit. The prisoners were separated. General Sandino and his aides were taken to a lonely spot at the airport, machine-gunned, and secretly buried under the runway. The father and the cabinet official were put into the military prison.

At about eleven, Ambassador Lane, still at work at the embassy, heard a burst of machine-gun fire in the city. Attempting to phone for information, he found the wire cut.

Driving, he located the shooting site and learned there had been an assault on the house of the Sandino party. Several had been slain, including a brother, Socrates Sandino. The Guardia officer pleaded self-defense to Lane.

The troubled ambassador next contacted the president. When Sacasa begged Lane to come to the palace, he did so immediately. Sacasa knew that the Guardia had taken his departing guests, and nothing more. His attempts to phone General Somoza had failed. Sacasa and friends were quaking with fear. They supposed they were the next targets in a revolution, and implored Lane to find Somoza and bring him to the palace. The ambassador would be safe, for he was an American.

It was about one o'clock as the "noninterventionist" U.S. envoy drove to Somoza's heavily guarded residence. He demanded to see Somoza, and the general appeared fully dressed. He claimed to have been at a poetry recital all evening. But this was not the cocky, confident Tacho. He too was fearful—for his life if he left the house. But Lane ordered him into the auto and they drove to the palace, where Somoza, lying, said he knew nothing about the fate of Sandino, but did reveal that the father and cabinet minister were lodged in the military prison. Continuing in his role of helpless onlooker, Tacho said he could not be held responsible for their fate.

So envoy Lane was again induced to intervene, this time out of mercy. In a foul mood he drove to the prison and by carrying on like a violent American imperialist secured the release of the two prisoners and took them to his home for safety. The writing of an explanatory cable to the State Department completed the long night of Arthur Bliss Lane.

This was not a revolution; it was Sandinista extermination as the Guardia unleashed a massacre in General Sandino's settlements. The survivors were scattered and hunted down over the next two years. Sacasa ordered a complete investigation of the political murders of February 21, but it was paper bluster. He had no power. Juan Sacasa would sit in the president's chair only so long as Somoza willed it.

Soon the killers boasted of their deeds and displayed grisly souvenirs, gold teeth whacked from Sandinista skulls. It is not known whether the murder of Sandino was proposed by Somoza, or if he went along with pressures within the Guardia. Moncada applauded the killing of his old enemy, and Somoza hinted the lie that Ambassador Lane had approved the execution. The martyrdom of General Augusto Cesar Sandino became a lasting sensation throughout Latin America, where many believed, and believe today, that the United States was at the bottom of it. But the anti-intervention turn of mind within the State Department in 1934 was so negative and distant that in Nicaraguan policy making (if there was any) the planners overlooked Sandino, a leftover personality from a past best forgotten.

Somoza allowed Sacasa to linger in office until the spring of 1936. Tacho recalled the fate of General Chamorro, who never obtained U.S. recognition, and so, withering, had to give up the presidency. The Americans were stuffy about revolutions and trampling on constitutional laws. So there was considerable maneuvering to be done, and Sacasa was allowed to continue—even after a clumsy assassination plot against Tacho was uncovered, its roots trailing toward Señora Sacasa's political circle.

The thing to do was to secure control of the congress and have it rewrite the national laws to suit Somoza's purpose. This occurred in 1935. In 1936 the squeeze was applied. Riots (incited by guess who?) erupted in Managua, but the Guardia didn't move, at first. Sacasa couldn't quell the uproar, and the Guardia pressed for his resignation as a matter of public safety. It was easy: Sacasa "is so nervous he can't talk coherently," reported the U.S. envoy. "He insists on only one thing, getting out of the country alive."

The Guardia was the culprit, but not Somoza—Tacho had (temporarily) resigned! The Nicaraguan congress, after the vice-president was also induced, perhaps by bribe, to quit, elected a Somoza lackey who served until the "legal" election, in the fall, of General Anastasio Somoza.

Tacho was on top, but not yet satisfied. He resigned, had the constitution rewritten for an eight-year presidential term, again presented himself as candidate, and was elected with 99 percent of the vote. By similar constitutional manipulation and trickery he would clutch the levers of power for nineteen years and get on splendidly with the Americans nearly all of the time.

President Somoza pressed his ploy of making up to the Americans. One of his early moves was to declare a two-day holiday when Franklin D. Roosevelt was reelected in 1936. And in 1939, the year that Tacho fixed his long electoral term, his image in the States was promising, as news heads from the *New York Times* index show: Somoza— inaugurates first twelve houses for government workers . . . announces stamps in honor of Will Rogers . . . prepares for tourist traffic . . . praises Roosevelt's peace appeal to Hitler and Mussolini . . . becomes master mason . . . says Nicaraguan canal will be built . . . expels Nazi who jilted Nicaraguan girl . . . gets baseball team equipment from Mayor LaGuardia . . . opens Managua health clinic . . . and so on. An accumulation of these gestures secured for him the prized invitation of an official visit in May 1939 to Washington, D.C. Its extravagance was a caudillo's impossible dream come true!

A special train carried President and Mrs. Somoza from New Orleans into the U.S. capital. President and Mrs. Roosevelt, the vice-president and his wife, the chief justice of the Supreme Court, and nearly every cabinet member *came to the station* to greet the Nicaraguans. (Was William Walker spinning in his grave?)

The top-hatted presidents shared an open limousine in

the midst of a military cavalcade: fifteen tanks in front, fifteen more behind, with five thousand servicemen lining the route, and behind them a thick belt of government workers who had been encouraged to look on. Overhead droned a large portion of the prewar Army Air Corps: ten new B-17 Flying Fortresses and a swarm of fighter aircraft. Tacho was honored at a sumptuous state dinner, slept one night in the White House, addressed the U.S. Congress, and went on as a privileged tourist to see the New York World's Fair. Who could ask for anything more?

Well, there were qualifiers. Somoza's grand reception had been laid on as a dress rehearsal to eliminate any wrinkles before the main event: The king and queen of England were coming to Washington. Also, the Americans tried to stress that Somoza's welcome was representative of sentiments due to *all* of the "Good Neighbor" nations to the south. Nonetheless, Somoza returned south as the blue-ribbon Latin American leader. His friends and enemies at home and in neighboring nations clearly saw that. And Tacho never allowed them to forget it!

After reading a State Department paper detailing Somoza's rise to power, President Roosevelt supposedly remarked, "He's a son of a bitch but he's ours." Indeed Tacho had pledged: "I consider every Nicaraguan aviator and soldier as a potential fighting man for the United States." And when Pearl Harbor dashed the United States into World War II, Nicaragua followed immediately, with the U.S. grateful for Tacho's avid support when Nazi submarines prowled the Caribbean in 1942.

Anastasio Somoza was Nicaragua's second caudillo, after Zelaya, whose get-rich methods Tacho savored. But he avoided his predecessor's major mistake of riling the Americans. Somoza well understood the postintervention U.S. attitude—never get mixed up in that country again! So he offered complete cooperation in any errand the United States called him to, and in exchange the Americans allowed him to operate in his nation as he pleased. This implicit agreement survived until about 1978.

The dictator shrewdly understood the advantages of window dressing for foreign eyes. Somoza's dictatorship was not as obviously brutal as others. "I know every man in Nicaragua and what he represents," boasted Tacho. Because it looked good, he could and did allow political opposition so long as it was futile. For varying periods newspapers got away with denouncing the regime shrilly, and speakers harangued against Somoza. But whenever the watchful caudillo believed that someone was gaining on him, then came exile, or imprisonment and perhaps selective torture. The Somoza specialty was a wire circlet about the scrotum lightly electrified.

"Oh, hell, that damned thing isn't so bad," claimed Tacho. "I've tried it myself—on my hand."

Equaling the vanity of indulgence in absolute power was the Somoza passion for self-enrichment. Like Zelaya, the Somozas made Nicaragua into a family monopoly. They accumulated business licenses and sold them at a handsome profit, and purchased or confiscated many businesses themselves. And land! Tacho's favorite pose was to present himself as a farmer patriotically called away to national purpose. His approach was direct: Contact the landowner and offer (demand) to buy his property. Usually the Somozas offered one-third to one-half of its market value. By the end of the Somoza era there was credibility to the saying: Somoza owns a hacienda down south; it's called Nicaragua.

Even international events favored the grasping Tacho. For example, when Nicaragua declared war on the Axis powers, who pocketed their seized assets? And who sold land and supplies to the U.S. military forces when bases were established in the nation during World War II? Of course the Nicaraguan economy improved under Somoza's stability and opportunism, but his family's economy improved even more. Estimates of the Somoza fortune, in the mid-1950s, ranged from sixty to one hundred million dollars.

President Somoza did get into official trouble once with the Department of State during the Truman administration. Around 1948, during one of his constitutional acts of self-perpetuation, Tacho installed an aged puppet who unexpectedly tampered with the Guardia and even censured Tachito, a Somoza son and heir. Papa had his congress declare the upstart president mentally incapacitated and put in his place another stooge. The stink of the affair rose internationally and the United States virtuously withheld recognition of the arrangement, but softened after several months.

According to Tacho, they just didn't understand conditions in Nicaragua: "Democracy down here is like a baby and nobody gives a baby everything to eat right away. I'm giving them liberty—but in my own style. If you give a baby a hot tamale, you'll kill him."

In 1946 Somoza's country switched, in cadence with America, from anti-Nazi to anti-Communist. So in 1954, the Eisenhower administration asked Tacho's aid in overturning a troublesome regime in Central America. The Dulles brothers, John Foster as secretary of state and Allen as CIA director, perceived a shocking pink in the political complexion of President Jacobo Arbenz's regime in Guatemala. A change of government was desirable and accomplished with Nicaragua pleased to provide a base of covert operations.

There is a story that when Tachito, the youngest Somoza, returned from long U.S. schooling, a temporary perspective gained during three years at West Point provoked a complaint to his father about the family image. Dictatorship was out of style, said Tachito, and people really didn't care for the Somozas. He thought his family had gathered plenty of money, so why not go away and live it up in some civilized land? Tacho reacted harshly; he threatened to court-martial the young captain. Yoya, Tachito's mother, is recorded as saying that she would rather be the widow of the president than a wife of an exile.

Fueled by greed and pride of place, Somoza proceeded unheeding until a fateful public party in León on the evening of September 21, 1956, in his sixtieth year. When the festivity had reached saturation level, a young, moralist poet walked up unaccosted and fired four bullets into the beefy dictator. Rigoberto Lopez Perez was belatedly riddled by the presidential bodyguard.

Somoza still lived and the Americans arranged his air transport to their hospital in the Canal Zone. President Eisenhower, expressing shock and anguish, sent his personal surgeon to be in attendance. But to no avail: "I'm a goner," Tacho confided to the U.S. ambassador, and in seven days he went. Somoza's fatal mistake was in lingering too long at his vulgar banquet.

U.S.–Nicaraguan events of the period are too close to us in time to be the subject of reasoned historical analysis. Informed, dispassionate appraisals have yet to be written about the fall of the Somozas or the coming to power of the Sandinistas and their confrontation with the USA. Contemporary accounts are often impressionistic and passionately anti/pro, meant to sway opinion or justify events rather than to record and explain them. The rest of this book is inevitably affected by these factors.

The two Somoza sons had been groomed for leadership and Luis assumed command. He was the most liberal Somoza, ruled only one term as he promised, and then retired behind a hand-picked choice, Rene Schick Gutierrez. Restraint on the media was somewhat loosened, the Guardia more discreet in its police functions, but the junior Somozas served up no "hot tamales" of liberty either.

In 1961 the Somozas again assisted the United States (the

Kennedy administration) in the attempted overthrow of a Latin American government. Forces of the botched "Bay of Pigs" operation against Castro's Cuba trained in Nicaragua and departed for action from there. In response, in Cuba that year, a tiny guerrilla group was formed. It was a Marxist reincarnation of Sandino's organization. But the Sandinista National Liberation Front (FSLN) was not a factor of political or military importance in anti-Somoza activity for a dozen years.

Tacho II (formerly Tachito) was eager for his turn at the top, and as Luis died of natural causes in 1967, he was the sole dictator in fact for the next dozen years. Tacho II lacked the soft-soap touch and innovative style of his father. Consequently he was perceived as a brutal overseer of corruption, the dictator people loved to hate. Over the years, that came to mean just about everyone except his dependent associates and the very powerful (through U.S. aid and military instruction) Guardia. The Guardia owed its identity to the Somozas and settled in as an army of occupation in its own nation.

Tacho II apparently considered himself an Americanized imperialist (he said that Spanish was his second language) residing in Latin America to squeeze a personal fortune out of a backward country. He demanded, took for granted, U.S. support, saying: *My enemies are yours, too.* And he wrote a book at the end, *Nicaragua Betrayed.* Tacho II blamed the United States.

The United States did vigorously support the last Somoza, particularly during the Nixon administration. There was a U.S. ambassador in that period, Turner Shelton, who was close to Tacho II: "I think President Somoza is a very nice man . . . he does a good job and he's a hard-working leader who has done a lot to improve things in this country." Shelton was of the opinion that if a U.N.-governed election were held in the land Somoza would win easily.

On December 23, 1972, an earthquake destroyed most of the capital. And again a natural event figured in Nicaraguan politics, for the shock of the quake revealed the evilness of the Somoza regime. The government handled the disaster (10,000 were killed) very poorly. The Guardia, responsible for public order, reacted in selfish panic and ran away or concentrated on caring for their own families. But Tacho II topped this, it is charged, with shamelessly manipulating the aftermath for personal enrichment. For example, the Somozas owned the only cement factory in Nicaragua. So the dictator ordered that most of the reconstruction must utilize that material. Also, according to journalist Stephen Kinzer, the entire U.S. Agency for International Development (AID) reconstruction grant of $3 million was used to buy a piece of land that Somoza had just purchased for $30,000! And no housing had been built there in the five years preceding Kinzer's 1977 article in *New Republic*.

Nicaraguan business interests had reasonably strong stomachs. They understood about taking commercial advantage, but the Somoza family was too pervasive, crowding them unheedingly out of all marketplaces. So the merchant middle class turned against the regime, joining the politically disaffected professional classes. But in contentious Nicaragua the usual result came about: disunity. The only middle-class agreement was in not desiring the Marxist faction to triumph alone. At this time, however, the FSLN Sandinistas, organized in Cuba in 1961, were themselves divided into three or four parts. So the bloated, obsolescent Somoza regime, propped by the powerful Guardia, was able to linger on for seven years. U.S. attitudes and actions, or lack thereof, also influenced the delayed collapse.

Nicaraguans clung to the notion that whenever a crisis arose in their governing process, the Americans would do something about it. The situation was terrible by the mid-seventies, and so they expected U.S. attention. When the

Carter administration critically looked at human rights under the Somoza rule and reduced military aid, saying uncomplimentary things about the way Tacho II governed, the opposition waited for the easy way to power. President Jimmy Carter would tell Somoza to leave.

Departure was suggested, but Tacho II was stubborn, insisting on remaining till 1981 when his "elected" term expired. The U.S. did not press him for years because there was disagreement about procedure and results. Some officials wanted Somoza out right away on grounds of moral principles. But others adhered to the "he's ours" doctrine. They pointed out that the FSLN Sandinistas displayed the most military clout, and therefore appeared to be the likely successor. Did the U.S. want a bunch of Communists running Nicaragua? No! It would be best if the current regime continued, somehow liberalized and without the Somozas. So they temporized for years, not knowing how to accomplish this objective.

When Tacho II made some mostly cosmetic changes to improve his international image, President Carter was sufficiently impressed to write the caudillo a personal letter, in June 1978, encouraging him in these efforts. It was of course leaked as evidence that Somoza was supported by the president of the United States. The anti-Somoza spectrum was dismayed. They realized now that they would have to do the job themselves.

The Guardia had whipped the new Sandinistas in early engagements in the old Sandino area and elsewhere. Then the FSLN established an urban guerrilla branch, which had two great hostage-taking public relations coups. In 1974 high-level guests at a reception for Ambassador Shelton were captured after the American had departed. It was like the Rivas gang affair fifty years before, but a bit bloodier. Somoza agreed to substantial demands of money ($1 million), prisoner release (including Daniel Ortega, veteran Marxist

FSLN leader destined for a top role in the coming Sandinista government), and propaganda broadcasts. It really improved the Sandinista image. And in 1978, they topped this by capturing the National Palace, including the sitting congress of Nicaragua. Again Tacho II caved in to ransom demands.

The foundering government contributed independently to its putrid reputation. Pedro Joaquin Chamorro, best known vocal Samoza opponent and editor of *La Prensa* newspaper, was murdered by a hit squad in January 1978. Bill Stewart, an ABC television reporter, was executed on camera by a Guardia unit in June of the following year. The film was sent back to the USA and shocked Americans even as the lying Somoza regime was calling it an FSLN outrage.

Toward the end, the FSLN was greatly bolstered by Fidel Castro when he saw that they surely had a chance to overturn Somoza, and the middle class, opposed to Somoza, also warmed to the Sandinistas when they realized that the FSLN might win on their own. Yet it was the FSLN's politicizing of Nicaragua's youth from all classes that brought the conflict to open civil war. They were idealistic and brimming with bravado, pledging not to compromise their liberty as their parents had done. Young Nicaraguans believed that they could make a big difference in their lifetime.

Sporadically, country areas or even major cities would be captured by the revolutionists, and then the better-equipped Guardia brutally would hammer back, not sparing the populace, wrecking and killing by artillery, tanks, bombers, nighttime execution squads, as if they were invaders from an alien culture and not fellow Nicaraguans. In the eleventh hour, amid rivers of blood (up to fifty thousand died), the Americans belatedly convinced Tacho II to depart on July 17, 1979—to Miami, where he was *not* welcome, on to the Bahamas, and finally to Paraguay, where another caudillo, Alfredo Stroessner, securely ruled. But it was no secure hiding place for Tacho II. On September 17, 1980, a terrorist hit squad lurking in Asunción, the Paraguayan capital, fired rockets and a hail of bullets into Somoza's white Mercedes and killed the exiled dictator.

In Nicaragua, a provisional government ruled while the terrible economic and social mess the Somozas left behind was afforded emergency attention. Temporarily, Daniel Ortega was the sole Sandinista member of the junta in power. But he had allies, and the FSLN owned the new military muscle in the land. The USA faced reality: The Marxist-oriented government that they had least desired was ruling Nicaragua.

# AFTERWORD

## *Back to the Future?*

COMPLETING AN ABOUT-FACE in policy, the Carter administration bravely smiled upon the Sandinista masters of Nicaragua, laid on $75 million in aid and loans for the devastated country. It was hoped that this money, and the prospect of getting more, would weaken their Communist alignment. Fidel Castro, the Sandinistas' teacher, urged the new leadership to avoid diplomatic isolation. They succeeded in the beginning to the extent of amassing $1 billion in aid worldwide. So the Sandinista response to the U.S. could be and was rather cool: *Thank you very much. We desire proper relations, of course, but not at cost to our plans of recasting Nicaragua as an* independent, *nonaligned nation, or to our friendship with other nations of our choosing.* An indicator of Nicaraguan preference in foreign allies appeared when the U.S. proposed to furnish military advisers as in the Somoza past. The offer was declined; instead two hundred Cuban military advisers were taken into Nicaragua.

Internally the FSLN-dominated government was concerned with three priorities. The most urgent, they believed, was to prepare for expected invasion from the outside. In Nicaragua attempted revolution is always being plotted somewhere, and former Guardia personnel were thick in Honduras and Costa Rica. The Sandinistas stressed a high level of attention and efficiency in their armed forces, and also looked after security along the alien east coast, where revolutions often began and were easily reinforced. Suspecting the loyalty of the Miskito Indians, the FSLN forcibly relocated about twenty thousand of them, violating their human rights but strategically removing them from access to the Honduras border.

The other two objectives were linked. First, get rid of non-Sandinista participation in the postrevolution government, and then reduce the middle class to an insignificant political factor; for the campesino, the common man, must be politicized for the Sandinistas. Instead of letting him stand by in the dust ignorantly watching the tramp of endless revolutionary armies (and being conscripted therein), they must kindle and harness the peasant's own political awareness. If all the previous Nicaraguan governments were run for the benefit of 5 percent of people, let the Sandinistas become a bastion supported by 95 percent of the people! To that end a literacy campaign was started and schools and public health centers expanded. Other benefits to Nicaragua's large underclass included mandated wage increases and land distribution and a 50 percent reduction in rents. Though progress might be fitful, the people would be convinced that their regime was trying to help them and therefore be supportive of it.

This radical political realignment, if carried through for a generation, would be a remarkable watershed in Nicaragua's history. The devastating revolution-to-revolution cycle of Conservative-Liberal belligerence would cease and long-term stability replace it.

It was the alleged export of revolution and its hardware

to El Salvador, hotly denied by the FSLN, that disillusioned the Carter administration and infuriated the incoming Reaganites. They immediately set out to destabilize the Sandinista regime in the old-fashioned way: Round up the opposition, arm and train them, and support the "Contras" in transborder raiding or hoped-for full-scale invasion. The Reagan administration's vigor was restrained by a substantial anti-intervention bloc in Congress and U.S. opinion.

A tendency toward repetition in events has been noted throughout the record of U.S.–Nicaraguan relations. Will the past continue to repeat itself in the future? Will the United States again strike out at a "Tar-Baby" grown bigger and stickier?

# SUGGESTED READING

*Nicaragua: A Country Study* (compiled for U.S. Army), 1982. Recommended as the best overall study of Nicaragua, historical and contemporary. Presented from a U.S. viewpoint but quite evenhanded in judgments.

*Nicaragua in Perspective,* Eduardo Crawley, 1984. Excellent historical review of Nicaragua from the viewpoint of a Latin American journalist.

*Manifest Destiny Denied,* James T. Wall, 1981. Knowledgeable survey of U.S.–Nicaraguan relations from Monroe Doctrine through Walker's filibustering.

*Filibusters & Financiers,* William Scroggs, 1916, 1969. The standard reference source for the period up to 1900.

*The Nicaragua Route,* David I. Folkman, 1972. Fine detail on the whys and why-nots of the Nicaraguan Canal.

*Freebooters Must Die!* Frederic Rosengarten, 1976. Best writing on William Walker. Superbly illustrated.

*Dollar Diplomacy,* Scott Nearing, 1925, 1970. Well-written, and critical, estimate of this U.S. interventionist ploy.

*Banana Gold,* Carleton Beals, 1932, 1970. Impressionistic memoir of the author's journey to Nicaragua and meeting with General Sandino.

*The Sandino Affair,* Neill Macaulay, 1967. Much detail, particularly on guerrilla-Marine tactics.

*Time* (cover story), November 15, 1948. Eye level, memorable profile of Tacho I.

*Guardians of the Dynasty,* Richard Millett, 1977. Best scholarly appraisal (to about 1972) of the Somozas.

*Somoza and the Legacy of U.S. Involvement,* Bernard Diedrich, 1981. Journalistic impressions of Tacho II's overthrow and the new Sandinista government.

# INDEX